WILDERNESS
JOURNEY

Front Cover: Ian and Sally Wilson canoeing on Lake Winnipeg.
Back Cover: Travelling by dog team and carriole toboggan in northern Saskatchewan.

Our sincere thanks to:

Altamira Investment Services
Molson Breweries
The North West Company
The Royal Canadian Geographical Society

for their generous support
of our voyageur expedition

WILDERNESS JOURNEY

Reliving the Adventures of Canada's Voyageurs

Text and Photographs by
Ian & Sally Wilson
Illustrations by Sally Tatlow Wilson

Gordon Soules Book Publishers Ltd.
West Vancouver, Canada
Seattle, USA

Published in Canada by
Gordon Soules Book Publishers Ltd.
1359 Ambleside Lane
West Vancouver, B.C. V7T 2Y9
(604) 922-6588 or (604) 688-5466
fax: (604) 688-5442
email: books@gordonsoules.com
web site: www.gordonsoules.com

Published in the United States by
Gordon Soules Book Publishers Ltd.
PMB 620, 1916 Pike Place #12
Seattle, WA 98101-1097
(604) 922-6588 or (604) 688-5466
fax: (604) 688-5442
email: books@gordonsoules.com
web site: www.gordonsoules.com

Canadian Cataloguing in Publication Data
Wilson, Ian, 1955–
   Wilderness journey

   Includes bibliographical references and index
   ISBN 0-919574-74-2

   1. Wilson, Ian, 1955– —Journeys—Canada. 2. Wilson, Sally, 1955– —Journeys—Canada. 3. Frontier and pioneer life—Canada. 4. Canoes and canoeing—Canada. 5. Dogsledding—Canada. 6. Voyageurs.* 7. Canada—Description and travel. I. Wilson, Sally, 1955- II. Title.
FC75.W56 2000   917.104'648   C00-910859-9
F107.W56 2000

Edited by Anne Norman
Cover design by Harry Bardal
Printed and bound in Canada by Transcontinental Printing

C O N T E N T S

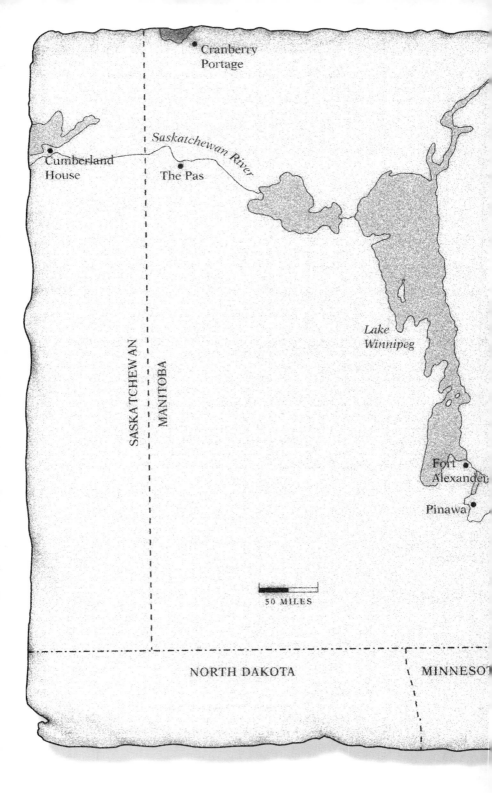

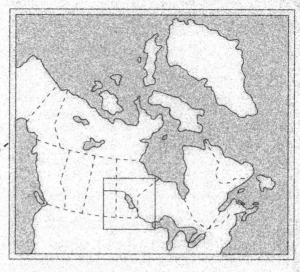

N

ONTARIO

Canoe Route
— from —
Grand Portage
— to —
Cumberland House

Winnipeg River

• Kenora

*Lake of
the Woods*

*Rainy
Lake*

Fort
Frances •

Thunder
Bay •

Grand
Portage •

*Lake
Superior*

N.W.C°.

Witness All Present That the assignee by these presents

Jean Baptiste Lavalée

does voluntarily engage and

In the presence of

Alexander Henry the younger

Accepts these terms of

The North West Company, to be employed as

Canoeman / Dog driver for three years in the northwest

And;

to winter at Cumberland House

And that **Jean Baptiste Lavalée**

Obliges and promises to conform to the ordinary wage of the voyage, and will comport himself as a good and faithful worker, obeying any representative of the said Company, and will not trade on his own account, nor absent himself nor quit the service or suffer the penalties set down by the laws and ordinances of Lower Canada, and will not be free from this engagement until his return to:

Montreal

For this engagement to be paid the sum of:

1400 livres

in Grand Portage Currency

With this Equipment:

1 capot, 2 vests of corduroy, 2 pair of trousers, 2 silk handkerchiefs, 2 cotton chemises, 1 three point blanket, 2 carrots of tobacco, 1 pair of beef shoes, and 1 tumpline

Signed and Passed on **2 July**

In the year seventeen hundred and **ninety seven**

By **X**

And signed with the exception of said Engagé who hath declared that he cannot read nor write, hath heard and understood this contract and hath made his usual mark.

Witnessed by

Daniel Francis Mackenzie

*A contract that a would-be voyageur
might have signed two centuries ago.*

The Voyageur Spirit

The bow of our canoe plunged into a boiling cauldron of whitewater, drenching Sally from straw hat to moosehide moccasins. Red paddles flashed in the sunlight and the roar of rapids filled the air. We strained against the current of Gunflint River, which forced the thin hull of our canoe towards dark, looming rocks.

Sally steered the canoe hard right. Knees braced against the gunwales, I leaned into my paddle to follow her lead. A black form streaked across my peripheral vision, but there was no time to contemplate how close the rock had been to the canoe. Our next challenge lay a heartbeat downriver.

We negotiated another boulder-strewn stretch of whitewater before the current slowed and we pulled into an eddy to rest for a moment. Clutching my paddle, I contemplated the river. Here we were in a birchbark canoe, deep in the wilderness, on a year-long re-enactment of the life of voyageurs. As I gazed at the surging water, I wondered exactly how authentic I wanted our re-enactment to be.

The words of a fur trader written two centuries ago tumbled through my mind like waves on the river: "They were hurled down with surprizing velocity thro' three

9

successive cascades. The canoe was several times over-whelmed with water, and threatened every moment with being dashed to pieces under water. Then . . . the current drove it toward shore, with two men hanging after."

"Second thoughts?" Sally asked, bringing me to the present.

"A few. Somehow, boulder-gardens never seemed as daunting when we were in a fibreglass canoe."

"Just what I was thinking," Sally replied. Both of us were experienced canoeists, but had paddled only robust modern canoes before. Would our birchbark craft survive a single significant error? Would the thin cedar ribs break if we hit a boulder?

"Well, that's enough second thoughts for me—let's go for it!" I said a moment later, breaking into a wide grin. One reason for this journey was the thrill of tackling new challenges. And this stretch of whitewater looked as though it would test our skills to the limit. We dug our paddles into the river and hurtled towards the next rapids.

Our tumultuous ride down the Gunflint River in the Ontario wilderness had its beginnings more than a year earlier. On an overnight trip from Vancouver, Sally and I had been sitting beside a campfire, flipping through the musty pages of a book we'd found in a second-hand bookstore. As Sally read a passage from Alexander Henry's journal, the words had planted the first spark of an idea for our journey: "Beneath upturned canoes, or lying with their feet to the fire, the French voyageurs are found scattered about the camp. In the morning, one shouts lustily . . . and the motionless forms spring to their feet. The sun begins to glimmer above the horizon, the fog clears slowly away . . . and a cheerful day is begun."

"That sounds like my kind of trip! Can I have a look?" I asked, reaching for the book.

Alexander Henry was a fur trader and explorer who had travelled with the voyageurs. Although his journal was penned long ago, Sally and I identified with the sense of adventure that had inspired young men to leave farm life in

Quebec and paddle birchbark canoes across the continent. Fabulous tales told by returning voyageurs lured them to sign on with the North West Company, to carry trade goods west in early summer and return with furs in the fall.

Leafing through the book, I came to a vivid description of running whitewater and read it aloud. When I glanced up at Sally, her eyes were closed and she seemed to be in another place, another time.

"Ready to sign on as a paddler?" I asked.

"Got a quill pen?" Sally replied. "I'll mark my X now!"

Sally leaned over my shoulder, and together we peered at the small type by dancing firelight. That evening, we dreamed of following in the footsteps of the voyageurs. The idea wasn't that far-fetched. Many years earlier we had traded secure lives in the city for the challenge of wilderness life. In 1982 we quit our office jobs to take a path less travelled and fulfil our yearning for wild places.

Since then, we had built a log cabin in the northern woods, travelled by dog team across the frozen Arctic, and followed an old gold rush trail by horseback. Sally and I had slurped mosquitoes in our soup, waded through waist-deep swamps, and fallen through the ice on Hudson Bay, but had never looked back.

Between trips, we had scrimped together enough savings to finance our next expedition by writing, giving school presentations, and teaching outdoor programs. Our evening by the campfire, reading Henry's journal, was a brief respite from city life. As we sat by the fire, Sally and I felt the familiar yearning to return to the wilderness. We were looking for another challenge—and reliving the life of voyageurs had all the elements we sought.

Like the French-Canadian farm-hands, we talked of seeing new places, having new adventures, and enjoying the camaraderie of life on the trail. We imagined exhilarating rapids and wild rendezvous along the way. And, like those before us, we gave little thought to the arduous portages, rain, wind, and mosquitoes that would also be part of the journey.

In another part of Alexander Henry's journal, I came to winter and read a paragraph to Sally: "We had a most delightful beaten track on which our Dog Sleds came on full speed. We were able to travel with expedition, having most excellent dogs . . . and our sleds not much encumbered with provisions. We drove on briskly until sunrise. The noise of our bells, and the cries of the men and their dogs signalled our arrival at the fort."

"That's it!" Sally said as I finished reading the passage. We had often thought of travelling by dog team through the northern forest. Now, intoxicated with wood smoke and stories of grand adventure, Sally suggested that we spend a year reliving the life of voyageurs who had travelled the North Country through four seasons.

"Of course, rounding up large dogs for freighting and finding an old-style toboggan might be a bit difficult," Sally added.

I leaned forward, baited by the challenging tone in her voice. "A true voyageur would worry about that when he got there," I countered. Despite my ready answer, I knew there would be many such obstacles to overcome on our year-long journey.

Over the next weeks, Sally and I read up on the history of the fur trade and researched the routes that had been followed by canoe and dog team.

"You know, to really experience voyageur life we should use old-style clothing and equipment—right down to a birchbark canoe," I said, looking up from the book I was reading.

Sally quickly warmed to the idea, and we contacted several museum curators to see if they knew of anyone who still built these canoes. The process of transforming a birch tree into a canoe that would survive the rigours of rapids and long portages seemed daunting. In addition, we weren't sure if we would have enough time to build a canoe by ourselves and paddle all the way north in one summer.

A few months later we received a letter from one of the few birchbark canoe builders in Canada. Tom Byers in northern Ontario had learned of our plans and offered to share his knowledge with us. I had no sooner put down the letter, when I picked up the phone and called Tom. He was enthusiastic about helping us build a canoe for our long journey, and agreed to work with us the following spring. Call it serendipity, or whatever, but we are amazed at how often we manage to meet the right person at the right time. Connecting with Tom was the first step towards turning our dream into reality.

Now we began our preparations in earnest. In the hopes of augmenting our limited funds, I wrote letters to several companies requesting supplies or sponsorship. Because one purpose of the expedition was to gather material for school programs, we hoped some of the companies would see the educational merits of our project.

As Sally and I continued our research, we learned that voyageurs were literally the backbone of the fur trade. Their labour was required to move tons of cargo over a route that spanned more than three thousand miles. A demand for furs had been created by European fashion in the 1600s. Beaver furs were used to make felt for men's hats, and other pelts were used for hand-muffs, decorative trim, and other accessories.

By the late 1700s, two rival companies dominated the fur trade in Canada. The British-owned Hudson's Bay Company had a trading monopoly for the entire Hudson Bay watershed. In competition, the North West Company was a partnership of independent traders. From its headquarters in Montreal, a trading route reached across the Great Lakes, then followed inland rivers and chains of lakes to the northern plains and beyond.

A voyageur for the North West Company would have signed a contract stating, among other things, that he would "comport himself as a good and faithful worker" during his term of engagement. Each recruit was outfitted with two shirts, two pairs of trousers, and two large handkerchiefs. They also received a blanket and several pounds of tobacco, as well as the promise of liquor along the way.

It didn't surprise us that the clothing of the voyageur is no longer stocked on merchants' shelves. Luckily, we were able to find patterns for breech-front trousers, drop-sleeve shirts, vests, and blanket coats at museums and archives. The brightly patterned calico cloth for shirts and the wool corduroy for trousers were harder to find. The good news was that when we did find material, it was usually on the half-price tables.

"Hey, I found some tablecloth material you'd look good in," Sally called one afternoon from the depths of a discount bin. I wasn't sure a voyageur would be caught dead dressed in a tablecloth, but the *fleur-de-lis* pattern did look the part.

When Sally produced the first prototype of the old-style trousers we would wear, I tried them on. As I walked to the mirror, she burst out laughing.

"What's so funny?" I asked.

"Turn around so you can see—you have a bad case of baggy butt!"

There was so much room in the seat I could easily have stuffed in a pillow.

"I can't be seen in these!" I complained.

"Well, that was the style back then. Maybe I could modify them just a little," Sally offered.

By the third prototype, the trousers looked passable and Sally set to work making two pairs each. My contribution to the project was to make a selection of buttons from a deer antler. Finally, we sewed on the buttons and Sally modelled her trousers.

"I'm in trouble," she said looking down. The three front flaps of her trousers were held closed with cumbersome buttons.

"Look at how many buttons I'll have to fiddle with when I'm in a hurry. *Five!*" Sally said, groaning. I suggested that buttons were merely one of the hardships she would have to endure in re-enacting voyageur life.

Sally produced the shirts we would wear with no problems other than modifying the large-sized pattern to fit her small shoulders.

"I'm still not sure about the trousers, but I really like these shirts," she said. "They'll be cool and comfortable." The shirts had a generous fit with pleats across the back for ease of movement.

What I liked best was the design of the sleeves. They featured a triangular gusset at each armpit, a practical design for hard-working, perspiring paddlers. Like the voyageurs, we would each use one set of clothes for everyday wear and save the other for special occasions, such as a rendezvous.

Our next project involved researching the foods that voyageurs had eaten. We learned that pemmican had been a staple for northern paddlers, along with corn, wild rice, and flour. One recipe indicated that pemmican had been made from dried buffalo meat and suet, mixed together and stored in canvas bags.

However, a journal of an early trader raised some questions about the ingredients of this food. He wrote: "Pemmican is supposed by the benighted world outside to consist only of pounded meat and grease; an egregious error; for, from experience on the subject, I am authorized to state that hair, sticks, bark, spruce leaves, stones, sand, etc., enter into its composition, often quite largely."

We decided to leave out several of those ingredients, although Sally spent hours searching for suet to make the pemmican. Of several butchers she phoned in Vancouver, only one understood the importance of using that type of fat—any other fat would turn rancid after being mixed with the meat.

Making pemmican became a community effort, as it had centuries ago. Sally rounded up some friends for a pemmican party. She had already dried jerky until it was brittle, and now they put the jerky into a canvas sack and pounded it to a powder. Her friends politely claimed that the hour of smashing at a canvas sack with a hammer on the sidewalk was therapeutic. Then Sally rendered oil from the suet and worked it into the powdered meat. For some reason, her friends failed to see the therapy they would gain by participating in this smelly, sticky task.

Once Sally had formed the pemmican into snowball-sized lumps, we divided our canoeing rations in three. Like voyageurs before us, we planned to pick up our provisions along the way. In addition to the pemmican, we packed flour, corn, and lard. Biscuits, cheese, and a selection of dried fruits and vegetables completed our simple fare. Each box contained enough food for thirty days of travel.

"Do you think pemmican is on the list of hazardous goods for shipping?" I asked as we prepared to mail our food to points along our route.

"Only if they eat it!" she replied.

Just before sealing the boxes, I realized we'd forgotten an important item.

"How many kegs of rum should we pack?" I wondered aloud. From what I had read, a daily ration was doled out to motivate the paddlers.

"Will that be fifty-pound or ninety-pound kegs you'll be carrying?" Sally countered. I did convince her that a small flask was required, for historical purposes.

With our food organized, we turned to selecting equipment for the trip. Several of the old journals we had read contained detailed lists of supplies that had been used long ago. But where in the twentieth century could we find tin cups and whistles, flint and steel, a brass compass, or even a hand-wrought axe? After some investigation, we found catalogues catering to museums and people interested in historical re-enactments.

Because Sally and I were on a tight budget, we hounded second-hand stores for as many things as possible. In one shop I found a wool blanket that looked like it could have belonged to Alexander Henry himself . . . as well as several traders after him. It was red with a broad black stripe across each end, and if blankets could tell a story, this one surely had a tale to tell. The weave was tight from many washings, and the colour faded from years of use. Small black dots on one side indicated where sparks from a fire had landed. This blanket would be our sleeping robe.

I even managed to find an old-fashioned felt top hat in downtown Vancouver, of all places. It fitted me perfectly and ended the dispute as to who would be the "guide" on this trip and who would be a mere paddler. I had the hat! Sally settled for a straw hat similar to the ones the paddlers had worn.

The canvas wedge tents used long ago proved to be more difficult to find. In fact, even waxed canvas is an uncommon material in this day of nylon and plastic. When I did find some canvas it was much too thick for Sally's sewing machine, so I took a number of sketches to a tent-maker.

"No problem," he said, as if making a small canvas tent for would-be voyageurs was a standard order.

A week later, our tent was ready. The same day, our first shipment arrived from a mail-order supplier.

"A jaw harp," I called out, digging through the box then twanging an off-key version of "Alouette."

"That'll liven up our evenings by the campfire," Sally said, rolling her eyes. I assured her that music had been an important part of a paddler's day. A good singer or fiddler was a valued member of a crew, and was often paid extra for these talents.

My skill on the jaw harp would not have brought me any extra pay, even if I had signed a voyageur's contract. And so, though we had found much of the old-style equipment needed for our journey, we began to worry about our dwindling funds. After tallying the cost of our supplies, there was little left over to pay the canoe builder and purchase dogs for our winter trip.

Over the next weeks, we received the support and encouragement of several companies, and our journey became possible. Sally and I joined our pemmican-making friends for an expedition-launching party, and we consumed enough chocolate cake and ice cream to compensate for a year of trail rations.

Our final project was to collect maps for our summer and winter journeys. It was only when we had unfolded thirty maps, linking our canoe route through three rooms of our friend's house, that we fully appreciated the scope of our expedition.

"At one inch to four miles, we've got a long way to go," Sally said, as her fingers followed a blue line of lakes and rivers. From start to finish, our canoe route wound across the maps for more than thirty feet.

"Almost sixteen hundred miles," I confirmed after adding up the distances from each map. Much of the route was still wilderness—especially along the Boundary Waters Canoe Area and Quetico Park, set aside to preserve the historic river system of the voyageurs. I could almost hear the wavering call of loons and the low howl of wolves as we dreamed of the journey ahead.

The route of the voyageurs who wintered in the north began at Grand Portage, on the shore of Lake Superior. It followed the waterways west over a series of lakes and rivers to Lake of the Woods, then north along the Winnipeg River. The route continued north on Lake Winnipeg, then up the Saskatchewan River to distant forts in the north-west.

The route wasn't all water though. We calculated that along the way, there would be more than one hundred miles of portaging. Sally and I would have to leave Grand Portage by early July in order to reach Cumberland House in northern Saskatchewan before freeze-up. It was this challenge of paddling so far in one summer, and the thought of adventures along the way, that fired our imaginations.

However, as we studied the maps more closely, some doubts began to creep into our thoughts. Sally wondered if she would have the stamina for the many portages. I worried that we would have trouble navigating through the maze of islands that cluttered Lake of the Woods. And I secretly worried that, after paddling all the way north, we might not be able to find dogs for a winter journey.

The Voyageur Spirit

We pushed those thoughts aside, and by early 1998 our storage locker was filled to the brim with canvas tarps, cooking pots, packs, and other gear. Tumplines that we had fashioned from lengths of canvas lay on top of one pile. I put a strap across my forehead and leaned forward, imagining what it would be like to struggle across a portage with heavy bundles on my back, supported only by this tumpline. I'd find out soon enough.

Before long, spring came, and we heard the honking of geese heading north. Like the voyageurs centuries ago, Sally and I looked skyward to watch the migration, waiting eagerly for warmer weather. As soon as the waterways were open, we could begin our journey back in time to the days of birchbark canoes, red paddles, and songs that echoed across the water.

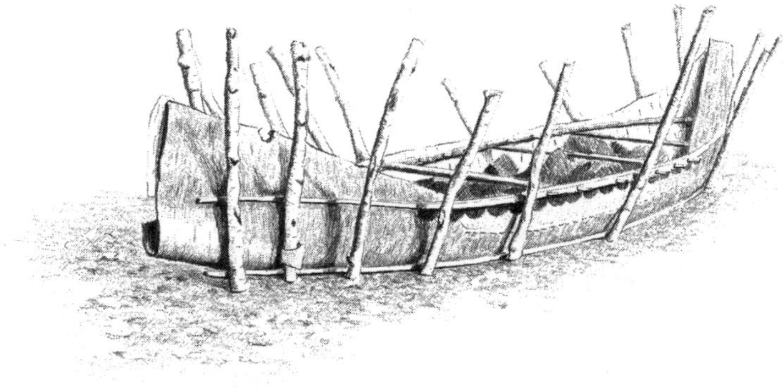

TWO

Building a Canoe

Like a vision from the past, a birchbark canoe and paddler approached through the mist of the cool, mid-May morning. With each silent dip of the paddle, the form drew closer. Sally and I waited expectantly on the shore of the Vermilion River near Sudbury, Ontario.

"Hi, folks, I thought I'd bring one of my canoes to give you an idea of what we're going to build." Tom Byers stepped into the water without letting the canoe touch shore. He had the lean, muscular build of a woodsman who spent his days swinging an axe and building canoes by hand.

After introductions, we pushed our fibreglass canoe into the river alongside his. Paddling beside Tom, we admired the sleek lines of his birchbark craft. By comparison, our modern canoe, loaded down with several weeks of provisions, looked rather utilitarian.

We made our way upriver to a small clearing, nestled in a forest of birch and spruce.

"Everything we need to make a canoe is in these woods," Tom said as we climbed up the bank from the river. "Birch, cedar, spruce root—even the gum to seal the seams."

In the centre of the clearing, Tom had fashioned a rustic workshop with a table made of poles, several stumps for splitting wood, and a hand-hewn bench. A length of carved cedar, surrounded by curls of wood, lay on the ground.

"What are you making?" Sally asked.

"Shavings." Tom smiled crookedly. He had been waiting for us to ask this question. With his dry sense of humour, I could tell we would enjoy working with him.

Then Tom showed us the tools that he used for canoe building. There weren't many, just an axe and a hatchet, a couple of crooked knives and awls, and a drawknife. A selection of clamps, a wooden mallet, and a splitting froe completed the collection. I found it amazing that a canoe could be made using only these basic tools. The fact that all the materials would come from the forest added to the mystique.

Around the campfire that evening, we told Tom more about our upcoming journey. As Tom became intrigued by our plans, I brought out my notebook and turned to the pages where I had copied some passages from old journals to take on our trip.

I read one of my favourites from the days of the voyageurs: "A push with the paddles, and the canoe shoots right down into the mad vortex. Then she steers right for a rock . . . on which it seems as if she would be dashed to pieces. A rapid turn of the bow paddle at the right moment, and she rushes past the black mass. The waves boil up at the side threatening to engulf her, but nothing gets in, and as she speeds into the calm reach beyond, all draw long breaths and hope that another rapid is near."

"You're planning to do that with your canoe?" Tom asked. A trace of a smile tugged at his lips, then he added in his understated way, "I think we'd better make the ribs extra strong."

With that thought, we headed into the forest the next morning to find the materials for our canoe. It took us a week to harvest birchbark and cedar, dig up pencil-thin spruce roots, and pick globs of gum off trees. By the time we had finished, our clothes smelled of cedar, musty earth, and spruce gum.

After hauling all the materials to camp, we spent the next days splitting cedar into thin slabs that we would fashion into ribs and other canoe parts. Then Tom carved a piece of cedar until it was a quarter inch thick, two inches wide, and four feet long.

"This will be our 'story-rib,' a sample for all the other ribs," Tom said, handing the length of wood to Sally.

Sally and I each selected a piece of cedar and began carving with crooked knives. Following Tom's example, Sally pulled the curved blade of the knife towards her. A sliver of wood curled from the cedar.

"The most important thing is to keep your other hand out of the way of the knife!" Tom reminded us, after glancing our way.

We each became absorbed in the task, concentrating on making smooth cuts with the knife. I soon realized it would take time to learn the nuances of this skill. With each draw of my knife I experimented with the angle of the blade and the amount of pressure I applied. Unfortunately, I often gouged the wood instead of carving off thin slices.

"How's this?" I asked Tom an hour later, proudly holding up my first rib. He looked at the crooked, hacked-up piece of wood and diplomatically suggested that it was quite good . . . for my first effort. We continued carving ribs for the rest of the day.

The next morning, Sally and I awoke to find our fingers frozen in the knife-gripping position. Sally giggled as we sat on our sleeping bag, prying our fingers open and then squeezing them closed.

"The good news is, I have no blisters," Sally said, comparing her hand to mine. "But I think I'll wear work gloves today, anyway."

For a change of pace, we took turns with the drawknife. Pulling the wide blade towards us, we fashioned long, thin sheets of cedar, called sheathing, that would be placed between the bark and the ribs in the canoe.

At one point, I paused in my work and looked across the work site. Not far away, Tom was using a mallet and froe to split a section of cedar. Sally sat cross-legged on the ground near the water's edge, covering herself with shavings as she carved a rib. Now and then, she paused to brush a mosquito from her face, adding shavings to her hair in the process. She looked quite comfortable and at home there, working and humming her favourite tune.

Over the next days while Sally and I continued carving the ribs and sheathing, Tom worked on more difficult projects. I looked up frequently to watch him split, then carve an awkward eighteen-foot length of cedar. This would become one of the gunwales, and I smiled, knowing I would appreciate the care he took each time I rested a hand on the upper edge of the canoe.

"A couple more days and we'll be ready to start building," Tom said when he'd finished carving the gunwale. "It's time to soak the birchbark in the river, so it will be pliable when we unroll it."

That evening, after submerging the bark in the river, we talked about our progress so far. It was early June and the work site was cluttered with the results of our labour: four dozen ribs, sixty lengths of sheathing, and four gunwales. Coils of spruce root and a pot of gum completed the raw materials we had gathered. We were just congratulating ourselves when loud splashing came from the river where we had left the bark.

"It's a beaver!" Sally exclaimed. "What if it eats the bark?"

I groaned, imagining beavers dining on the delicious dinner we had set out so conveniently for them.

"I can't imagine a beaver eating a tough old piece of birchbark when there's fresh aspen along the shore," Tom assured us, and laughed.

Even so, I was relieved when we hauled the unchewed

bark out of the river two days later. Working on hands and knees, the three of us carefully unrolled the birchbark onto a flat, sandy area we had prepared. We placed a canoe-shaped frame on top of the flattened bark, then heavy boulders on top of the frame to prevent it from moving.

After pouring scoop after scoop of hot water over the bark to make it pliable, we began folding up the sides of the canoe. Even though we'd been told that cuts had to be made in the bark to keep it from buckling, Sally and I gasped when Tom made a vertical slice in the bark.

"Want to give it a try?" he asked, offering his crooked knife. Although we were both eager to be involved in every step of canoe building, Sally declined.

"Don't worry, mistakes are what spruce gum is for," he said. Even with his assurance, I was nervous as I sliced the next gore. After one cut, I handed the knife back to Tom.

Seven cuts later, we hammered the last stakes into the ground to hold the bark in position. Then we sandwiched the bark between the inner and outer gunwales and drove in birch pegs to hold them together. For extra strength, we began lashing the bark to the gunwales with spruce root.

"Only seventy-nine to go," Tom said after he had completed the first lashing. Taking that as our cue to start on the other side, Sally and I drilled holes through the birchbark with awls, then lashed the bark to the gunwales.

"Can you help me tie this?" Sally called to me when she reached the end of her first lashing.

As I held the root, Sally looked up and our eyes met. I knew what she was thinking: working together, learning together, was what we enjoyed most. With teamwork, our dream to be voyageurs was one lashing closer to reality.

After two days of lashing, we helped Tom install the headboards and stem-pieces that would determine the shape of the bow and stern. Then, Sally and I poured pot after pot of boiling water over the ends of the gunwales while Tom carefully bent them upwards in a sharp curve.

When he was finished, the ends of the gunwales were nearly vertical, forming the final lines of the canoe.

"With a lot of hot water and patience, you can do almost anything with cedar," Tom said, smiling with satisfaction.

Now we were ready to lash the ends of the canoe closed.

"Make sure the lashings are really tight, otherwise your canoe will leak like a sieve," Tom teased as we began threading a long root through the bark.

"Pull!" I urged Sally as we crossed the root back and forth over the raw edge of the bark. The last thing I wanted was a canoe that leaked like a sieve! The time and care put into the canoe now would pay off during the rigours of travel. It would need to survive more than forty portages and many stretches of whitewater along the way.

June 16 was "rib day," the part of canoe building that Sally and I had most looked forward to. In preparation, we removed the boulders and the building frame that had been in the canoe from the beginning.

"It will float a lot better without this load of boulders," I quipped, tossing one aside.

"I was thinking we'd put them back in for ballast," Tom countered.

With the boulders and building frame removed, the envelope of bark now looked like a canoe. For the first time, I could visualize an express canoe of the fur trade, with a distinctive high, rounded bow and stern. This sixteen-foot-long canoe was designed for two paddlers and was used to take messages or an important passenger from one place to another.

The express canoe was the smallest of the voyageur canoes. Next in size were the North canoes, used to carry cargo west of Lake Superior. They were twenty-six feet long, carried three thousand pounds of cargo, and had a crew of six. And the largest were the Montreal canoes that plied the waters from Montreal to Lake Superior. They were thirty-six feet long, had a crew of twelve voyageurs, and carried an incredible six thousand pounds of cargo.

Bending the canoe bark to shape

Setting out the ribs

26

The best paddlers of the large canoes were chosen to paddle the express canoes. This had been a great honour for a voyageur. The express canoes were the North West Company's only means of communication during summer, and the emphasis was on speed rather than freight capacity. I daydreamed for a moment, thinking of the places that this craft would take us. The sound of Tom and Sally placing ribs across the gunwales brought me back to the present.

With forty-four ribs laid out like a cedar xylophone, we numbered each rib and drew pencil lines where they would be bent. After they were bent, the ribs would be placed inside the canoe and would determine the shape of the hull.

"Now for the fun part," Tom said, picking up a rib. After pouring hot water over the wood for several minutes, he sat on a stump and placed the rib across his knees.

"Put each knee at a pencil line and pull towards you," Tom said as he started bending the rib. I watched closely, noting that he poured hot water over the wood frequently during the bending process.

Tom bent several ribs to their U-shaped form before I took a turn. I was tentative at first, uncertain how much force might break a rib. However, I soon discovered that I had to strain to make any bend at all. Gradually, I applied more pressure . . . mindful that we had made only a few extra ribs.

CRACK!

I jumped, then let out a groan as Sally burst into laughter behind me. She had tiptoed close to me and broken a stick just as I was straining against the wood.

"Not a good idea to play tricks on the only person you'll be paddling with for three months," I taunted. I don't think Sally or Tom heard me over their peals of laughter.

I continued bending the rib, sitting by the hot fire, in the hot summer sun, pouring hot water over the wood. It was hard work. As soon as I had successfully bent several ribs,

I offered Sally a turn. She eagerly took her place at the stump as I slipped away to work on a cooler task.

I joined Tom as he fitted the bent ribs into the canoe. Rib by rib, the canoe began to take shape. The ribs would remain in place for a day or two until they were dry.

The next morning we began to prepare the gum that would be used to seal the seams.

"Watch it doesn't get too hot," Tom cautioned when Sally put the pot of gum over the fire.

"How will I know if . . . " Sally began, just as the contents burst into flames. She leaped up, fire and smoke billowing from the pot she held at arm's length.

"I'd say that's too hot," I said helpfully, as Sally madly blew on the flames. She shot me a glance that suggested she hadn't found my comment amusing. I brought her a stick so she could stir the gum, then left quickly before I was asked to take my turn by the hot coals.

When the gum had turned to liquid, Tom and I strained it through burlap to remove twigs, bark, and bugs from the brew.

"I bet porcupines would find this pretty tasty," Tom said as we stirred in bear fat to make a traditional canoe-gumming concoction.

With a straight face, Tom wondered aloud whether porcupines might chew the spruce-gum seams or even gnaw on our paddles and the gunwales for the salt left by our hands. He also suggested that if we left the canoe upside down on shore, a bear might mistake it for a rotting tree and tear it apart while searching for grubs.

"Maybe that's why voyageurs slept under their canoes," I said. "To fend off the beavers and bears!" But I wasn't worried about what might happen at night. It was the prospect of hurtling down rivers in a bark boat that raised my heart rate.

We helped Tom remove the ribs from the canoe two days later, so that we could apply spruce gum on the inside seams to seal the canoe before installing the ribs

Carving a gunwale

Bending a rib

Ready to install the ribs

29

permanently. Despite wetting my fingers, a good deal of the toffee-like spruce gum stuck to my skin. When I slapped a mosquito, my face and hair became gummed as well.

Sally wasn't doing much better. Her shirt stuck to the canoe when she leaned against it, and her hands became so covered in waterproof gum that her fingertips were glued together.

"Just chew it off with your teeth," Tom said. "It's like spruce-flavoured bubble gum!" Sally was not quite sure if Tom was pulling her leg.

"I think I'll make *galette* instead . . . that always gets my fingernails clean," Sally shot back with a mischievous grin. It was one of the few times Tom was speechless. He was probably thinking about the dough Sally had kneaded to make this voyageur-style flat bread earlier in the day.

Once we had gummed every possible place where the canoe might leak, we covered the inside of the canoe with thin sheets of cedar sheathing to protect the bark from the ribs. We were ready to permanently install the ribs.

Sally poured liberal amounts of hot water into the canoe to soften the bark and allow it to stretch. Slowly, carefully, Tom and I tapped each rib into place.

After a full day of installing the ribs, we had almost completed the canoe. The next day, we gummed the outside of the canoe, then, for a touch of luxury, Sally and I added seats. Many voyageurs had sat on bundles of trade goods, but the thought of sitting on lumpy pots and camping gear didn't appeal to us. Working from old drawings, we carved seats and suspended them from the gunwales using hemp cord Sally had braided.

"Let's launch it!" Tom said, the moment we tied the last knot.

As we would countless times in the coming weeks, Sally and I lifted the canoe to our shoulders. We guessed it weighed about ninety pounds. It didn't feel as heavy as I had thought it would, considering the thick ribs we had used. Then again, the cedar would probably soak up more water along the way, and our portages would be much longer than this one.

I held my breath in anticipation as we set the canoe down on the water. After five weeks of work, this was the moment of truth. The canoe floated serenely on the surface of the water, perfectly balanced from side to side. I was sure I heard Sally and Tom let out their breath at the same moment I did.

Tom tested the canoe first, paddling it down the river, rocking it from side to side, then putting it through manoeuvres. The smile on his face when he returned to shore said he was pleased with the way the canoe handled.

Sally and I waded into the river, then stepped into our canoe. At that moment, we stepped back in time, to an era when the birchbark canoe was the only means of transportation across this vast country. As I gripped my paddle, I felt the same excitement that a young French-Canadian farm-hand might have felt two hundred years earlier.

Our paddles entered the water in unison and the canoe glided smoothly across the river. It was wonderfully responsive, turning easily and sideslipping with little encouragement. It floated like a leaf on the water, more buoyant and more alive than any other canoe we had paddled. After putting the canoe through its paces, we approached shore wearing grins as wide as Tom's.

"It paddles like a dream!" Sally said as we glided to shore. We were in awe at how birchbark, cedar, and spruce root had been transformed into a finely crafted canoe. As the three of us sat on the bank of the river watching the canoe drift at the end of a rope, we talked of the journey of learning we had already taken, and the physical journey ahead of us.

Then, repeating a timeless ceremony of the voyageurs, I placed a red feather in the bow and another in the stern.

The feathers indicated that the canoe had been tested and found worthy.

The next day, Sally painted the crest of the North West Company on each side of the bow.

"Here's to a successful journey," I said when she had finished. We each raised a cup of tea, making a toast to the craft that would take us on the long journey from Grand Portage to the North Country.

THREE

Grand Portage

As Sally and I pulled on colourful calico shirts and buttoned up the breech-front trousers that she had sewn months earlier, we began to feel like voyageurs of days gone by. The transition felt complete when walked through the gates of the North West Company fort at Grand Portage.

"*Bonjour*, you must be the new voyageurs," a young man, dressed as we were, welcomed us. We wound our way past a large canoe and over to where he was chopping wood.

"And where are you headed?" he asked, noticing the paddle I carried.

"We're on our way to Cumberland House," I replied. He thought I was merely role-playing until I explained we really were paddling north. When I told him of our interest in the voyageurs, he offered to give us a tour of the fort.

After showing us around the compound, he left us at the Great Hall, where partners and agents of the North West Company held their annual meeting every July between 1784 and 1802. Inside the building, ledgers lay open on a table and quill pens were poised in ink-wells, as if the partners had just stepped out for a break.

Sally and I entered the company store and found a collection of mugs, sashes, tobacco, and other items a voyageur might need. Company stores did brisk business with the paddlers, especially those heading north for the winter. Sally bought a shiny tin mug, and I chose a bright-red ostrich feather for my hat.

"I can carry four bundles," I boasted to the clerk behind the counter. I remembered reading that bragging was normal behaviour for all voyageurs.

"Surely you are too modest," the clerk replied. "Most tell me they can carry six."

"Make your purchases and leave," another clerk interjected sharply, joining the charade. "I wonder why you voyageurs never wash."

Sally and I continued our tour to a cluster of canvas tents outside the fort. There, we joined two voyageurs by a campfire where a skillet of onions and potatoes sizzled over the red coals. The men were playing cards to pass the time but the scene was rather quiet compared with the dancing and drinking and brawling of two centuries ago.

"In the late 1700s, that beach in front of us would have been swarming with activity," one of the men informed us. "Brigades of Montreal canoes arrived every day. Imagine several large canoes racing to the beach, then the hustle and bustle of voyageurs unloading thousands of pounds of trade goods. They weren't given their ration of rum until the cargo was carried to the fort!"

He went on to tell us that from where we stood, we would have seen two encampments, one on each side of the creek. On the right would have been the men from the east—the Montrealers. On the left would have been the camp of the Northmen—the voyageurs who had arrived from the North Country. The creek was supposed to serve as a buffer to minimize fighting between the camps.

I thought of the Northmen swaggering around camp and bragging about their ability to paddle, dogsled, or drink. Between boasts, they would have hurled insults to the Montrealers across the creek. Late at night, they might have sneaked over to the other camp to ridicule and fight with the others.

After lunch with the modern-day voyageurs, Sally and I walked over to a collection of tepees on the opposite side of the fort. At this Ojibway village we met a young man dressed in buckskin. He was working on a birchbark canoe, held in position with stakes as ours had been. Several bent ribs lay beside the canoe.

We began talking about canoe building, and learned that during the days of voyageurs traversing the continent, native people had built seventy canoes here each year. The birchbark canoes of the fur trade were, except for minor stylistic changes, built exactly as native North Americans had built them for generations.

"Do you have supplies to repair your canoe?" he asked when we told him of our planned journey.

"We have a large piece of bark and a can of spruce gum," I replied.

"Roots?"

"No," Sally said, "we thought we'd just dig some up if we needed them."

"I'll be right back," he said, disappearing behind the shelter. He returned with two coils of spruce root.

"There's enough here for a couple of lashings," he said, handing Sally the root.

Over the centuries, the native people had been just as helpful to the traders and explorers as they travelled across the country. Among other skills, they had taught the Europeans how to build canoes, make pemmican, and survive in the wilderness. It seemed fitting that the young Ojibway man had helped us on our journey.

After two days at the fort, Sally was eager to begin our journey. "We should be going if we want to get to Cumberland House before freeze-up," she prodded. The next morning, we brought our canvas bags to the trailhead.

The strongest, toughest voyageurs who paddled the large canoes from Montreal to Grand Portage had been encouraged to continue north in smaller North canoes, winter over, and become Northmen. Sally and I were neither the strongest paddlers, nor the fastest, but we felt ready to tackle this challenge, starting with the *grand portage*, the big carry. It was named for the formidable nine-mile trail that leads from the fort to the navigable section of the Pigeon River. The portage was necessary to avoid a series of waterfalls and rapids as the river dropped to Lake Superior.

Sally and I stood at the trailhead with our packs, looking up the long climb with the same feeling of dread the voyageurs must have experienced. I grabbed a tumpline, placing the widest part of the strap across my forehead and draping the trailing ends over my shoulders. Sally heaved a bulky pack onto my back and tied the loose ends of the tumpline underneath.

"How's it feel?" she asked. My neck muscles bulged and my head felt like it was going to be pulled off my shoulders.

"A little back-heavy," I reported, leaning forward even more to counteract the weight that threatened to topple me backwards. Sally tied the tumpline shorter so the pack rested higher on my back.

"That's better," I decided, and tottered forward.

"Wait!" she said. "Voyageurs wouldn't have carried just one pack. Let me add another." She threw a small bag on top. I suppose I was not the first voyageur to wish he hadn't boasted so loudly back at the fort.

I staggered towards Sally. In my stooped stance, I somehow managed to heave her pack up and tie the tumpline under the load. We started up the trail.

Step by agonizing step, we climbed from the lake, bodies bent forward, straining against our tumplines. My only view was of my feet and the ground beneath them. There I saw a trail packed hard by thousands of moccasined feet tramping over it centuries ago.

The view at my feet did little to distract me from the misery of carrying a pack with only a tumpline. The canvas strap creased my forehead and cut into my shirt, chafing my shoulders. My neck muscles burned. When I hooked my

Visiting the voyageur camp

Tumping our load up the trail

37

thumbs under the straps to relieve the weight, my shoulders felt as though they would be torn from the sockets. Worst of all was the rigid position I was forced to adopt to carry the load . . . one stumble and I was sure I would fall face-first onto the trail.

"Rest stop!" I called out half an hour later. We dropped our packs and lay gasping on a bed of moss, contemplating the lot of the voyageurs. Now I knew why Alexander Henry had written: "The young men now began to regret that they had enlisted into this service, which requires them, as they say, to carry burdens like horses, when, by remaining in their own country, they might have laboured like men."

As we struggled over the trail, Sally and I took heart in the knowledge that the next longest of the many portages to come would be only two miles across. At least we weren't each carrying two ninety-pound packs, as many voyageurs had. They had said that it was easier to get to heaven than to the Pigeon River.

Eventually, the trail levelled off slightly and wound through the forest, past alternating pools of shade and sunshine. Slender shafts of light probed the overhanging branches and slanted through the tall columns of pine, dappling the time-worn trail. When I stopped to look up and admire the view, my load almost toppled me backwards.

After four hours of hiking we came to the old site of Fort Charlotte on the Pigeon River. Now, only a few earth mounds indicated where the fort had once stood. This had been the location of a storage depot consisting of a stockade, a few buildings, and an area where the canoes were kept while the Northmen went to the fort.

"Looks like the river has changed too," Sally mused as we gazed at the shallow, rock-strewn waterway. There was very little water coursing between the grassy, boulder-studded banks. Upstream, exposed rocks and riffles sparkled in the glancing rays of the afternoon sun.

Sally and I climbed down the grassy bank to check out the river. The water flowing through the narrow channel did not even reach our knees at the deepest places.

"Hardly enough water to float a duck, let alone our loaded canoe," I said. We decided to head back down the trail and start our journey where the Pigeon River drained from Fowl Lake.

"A week's ration of my chocolate if you carry all the packs to the fort!" I said to Sally.

"Only if you pay in advance," she replied. She knew as well as I did that the food pack was still at the trailhead.

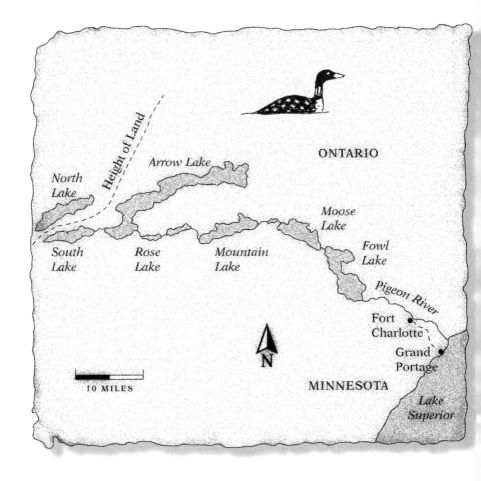

ONTARIO

Height of Land

Arrow Lake

North
Lake

Moose
Lake

South
Lake

Rose
Lake

Mountain
Lake

Fowl
Lake

Pigeon River

Fort
Charlotte

Grand
Portage

N

10 MILES

MINNESOTA

Lake
Superior

FOUR

To the Height of Land

A mountain of gear, including a canvas tent, five canvas packs, two boxes, extra paddles, and other assorted equipment lay heaped beside our canoe on the beach of Fowl Lake. Our canoe looked very small, and four weeks' worth of food and supplies looked very large.

"Think it will all fit in?" Sally asked. She steadied the canoe in the water as I carried the first pack from shore. The pack was so heavy, I was afraid I would drop it into our fragile craft.

"No problem, packing is my specialty!" I said confidently. Months earlier, I had calculated the volume and weight of supplies for each leg of our journey. However, lists and figures on paper were very different from the reality of cramming everything into the canoe. By the time we had loaded the canoe, it was bulging like an overstuffed suitcase. I was about to boast of my packing prowess when Sally pointed out that the canoe was leaning precariously to the left.

We spent half an hour rearranging the packs and boxes in different positions while standing knee-deep in frigid water. Finally, the canoe was loaded properly—balanced from side to side, and slightly stern heavy. The canvas packs were numbered as they would have been years ago, and I made a mental note of the placement of each one.

"It won't take as long next time," I said.

"That's lucky," Sally replied. "Otherwise we'd spend more time packing than paddling!"

As we stepped into the canoe, I calculated that our combined weight plus cargo added up to more than five hundred pounds. I recalled that Alexander Henry, after loading his canoes with kettles, lead balls, gunpowder, guns, and rum, had observed that "when all hands embarked, each Canoe sunk to the Gunnell." Suddenly, I knew how he must have felt as we started our journey with a seriously overloaded canoe.

Cautiously, we settled onto our seats, each holding our breath until the canoe had steadied. I was pleasantly surprised to find that we were not "sunk to the gunnell" after all. There was, in fact, plenty of freeboard at the centre of the canoe.

In unison, we dug our paddles into the calm water. It was July 4 and we were finally on our way. Our first resupply point was more than three hundred miles west at Fort Frances on Rainy Lake.

The canoe slid silently through the water, the ripple of our bow wave cleaving a perfect reflection of rock, trees, and sky. I breathed deeply, savouring the scent of sun-warmed pine. In the distance, I thought I heard the faint echo of voyageurs singing. Then again, perhaps it was just the gurgling of a creek or the wind whispering in the trees.

A splash from Sally's paddle jolted me out of my reverie a few strokes later.

"Sorry about that," Sally said, switching her paddle to the other side of the canoe.

A few strokes later, she splashed me again. "These paddles will take some getting used to," Sally said.

"Should I put on my raincoat until you get it right?" I teased. Actually, I was having some trouble with the long, thin blade of my old-style paddle as well. I did like the

Canot No. 25

Quantity				MEN'S NAMES, VIZ:	
N.W Mark	6	Bales	Trade Goods, No.s	Amable Lavalée	Guide
			C.H.# 4, 6, 11, 12, 13, 14	Jos. Le Tenne	2nd Avant
				Michel Viellette	Gouvernail
	1	Bales	Black Tobacco,	Antoine Le Fevre	Milieu, Cook
	1	"	Carrot Tobacco,	Pierre La Fontaine	Milieu
	1	"	N.W. Twist,	François Le Beuf	Milieu
	1	"	Copper Kettles,	Joachim Jourdain	Milieu
	1	Barrels	Salt,		
	0	"	Grease,		
	0	"	Powder,	PROVISIONS, VIZ:	
	1	"	White Sugar,	4 Bags	Flour,
	4	"	Lard,	2 "	Peas,
	4	"	High Wines,	2 Kegs	Grease,
	0	"	Rum,	4 Kegs	Lyed Corn,
	0	"	Spirits,	6 Sacks	Pemmican,
	1	"	Port,		
	2	"	Beef,		
	0	"	Butter,		
	1	"	Cheese,	EQUIPMENT, VIZ:	
	1	"	Raisins,	1 Ax,	
	1	"	Prunes,	2 Oil Cloth,	
	1	"	Figs,	1 Sail,	
				3 Lines,	
	0	Cases	Iron,	1 Kettle,	
	0	"	Knives,	1 Sponge,	
	0	"	Guns,	1 Awl,	
	1	"	Traps,	1 Roll Bark,	
	1	"	Soap,	1 Bunch Wattap,	
				6 Lbs. Gum,	
	1	Maccarons	High Wines,		
	0	"	Spirits,		
	0	Bags	Shot		
	0	"	Balls,		
	30	PIECES			

At: **Grand Portage,
2 June, 1797**

A bill of lading for a North canoe.

crimson-red blade, though. The blades had been painted red to preserve the wood and because voyageurs loved bright colours.

After talking it over, we concluded that instead of our usual paddling rhythm, we would need to adopt the short, quick strokes of the voyageurs. However, when Sally picked up the pace, I had difficulty keeping up.

"Could you slow down just a little?" I asked. To paddle efficiently, we had to be in unison, and I needed time to steer with my J-stroke. The customary forty-stroke pace of the voyageurs would take some time to work up to.

Eventually, we fell into a comfortable rhythm: paddles entering the water in unison and sweeping back together, a slight pause, then repeating the action. Every now and again, though, Sally increased the speed of her paddling until I had to ask her to slow down. I smiled to myself when I realized that it was the excitement of finally being on our way that was fuelling her paddling. With each paddle stroke, we were leaving the hustle of city life farther and farther behind us.

During a rest stop, we pulled out the maps to see what lay ahead. For the next few days our route would take us almost due west along a chain of ten narrow lakes, each linked by a portage to avoid stretches of impassable rapids. Many lakes had been named after the wildlife that voyageurs had encountered, such as Goose Lake, Moose Lake, and Rat Lake. Mountain Lake, Lily Lake, and Spruce Root Lake hinted at sights we might see along the way.

On our first day, we paddled as far as Mountain Lake. As the sun neared the horizon, we began looking for a place to make camp. Voyageurs surely had favourite stopping places, featuring sandy beaches where they could easily unload a canoe.

"You're the guide . . . where should we stop?" Sally asked as we looked down the lakeshore. It appeared to offer only a choice of steep bluffs or rocky bays. Not knowing if any better camping sites lay ahead, I suggested a small, rock-strewn bay that offered protection from any wind that might sweep down the lake.

"Let's jump out here," I said as we drifted into the bay. Tom's words about not letting the canoe touch shore were fresh in our minds. We splashed into knee-deep water.

Sally held the canoe while I lifted out the first pack. Picking my way across slime-covered, rounded boulders while wearing moccasins was like trying to walk across greased cannon-balls. With both hands occupied holding the pack it was hard to keep my balance as I slipped and slid towards the beach. Sally seemed to be enjoying the performance, however.

"You're lucky we have no *bourgeois* with us," Sally called, referring to the North West Company partners who often travelled in the canoes. "It would have been your job to keep his feet dry and carry him on your back to shore."

I pointed to my felt hat. "I doubt guides carried the *bourgeois.*" Besides, I reasoned, unless they were in a great hurry, the partners would have chosen a larger canoe to take them to the North Country.

Once our packs and the canoe were on shore, we began a camp routine that would be repeated every night for the next three months. First priority was to find a sheltered, relatively flat area for the tent.

"How's your side?" I asked Sally, as we lay on the ground to test our potential site.

"Lumpy. Can we move your way a bit?" she answered. Once we had cleared sticks and rocks and groomed our sleeping area, we set up the canvas tent.

While Sally began to cook supper, as well as *galette* for the next day, I stashed our gear under the canoe to keep it dry. Then I hung the food bags in a tree to keep them out of the reach of bears and other hungry creatures.

Finally, our chores completed, Sally and I sat by the campfire to eat. We gazed out over the sparkling water, drinking in the beauty of this wild place. Across the mirrored lake, pine-topped hills sloped gently down to the water. Billowing clouds rolled over the hills, glowing pearl-pink in the last warm rays of the sun.

The peaceful scene was broken by a loud yelp as I took my first sip of tea.

"*Maudit!* These tin mugs are hot!" I exclaimed, wiping a sleeve over my burnt lips. Ten sips later, the tea had cooled as the metal conducted the heat. Another ten sips and my tea was tepid.

The cold tea was flavoured with a distinctive tang of tin. It also dripped steadily from a flaw in the hand-soldered seam along the bottom.

"No wonder the voyageurs carved their own wooden cups," I said to Sally later, as I remelted the solder with the heated axe head.

"I like the tinware. It's kind of rustic," she replied, drying a metal plate over the fire.

I wondered whether she would like our sleeping accommodation as much as the tinware. Our tent was the size and shape of a Boy Scout pup-tent and seemed a lot smaller than it had at the tent-maker's. As we crawled into our shelter, we were greeted by the musty smell of waxed canvas. Pleasantly tired from our first day of travel, we settled down with wool blankets for warmth and a rolled-up canvas tarp for a pillow.

"I remember reading that paddlers slept only four hours a night," Sally murmured.

"I can sleep twice as long as any voyageur," I boasted just before I dozed off.

On our second day, we came to three short portages in a row. The lakes we crossed were little more than beaver ponds: glittering green dots in a landscape of poplar and spruce. We would load the canoe, paddle for a few minutes, then unload for the next portage. Each time, our routine of packing and unpacking became more refined. With thirty-six portages on the route to Rainy Lake, I had a feeling we would soon be experts.

We had a good chance to practise our portaging techniques a day later at the infamous Long Portage, a two-mile carry leading to Rose Lake. The path led over sharp rocks, through wet places, over windfalls and tangled roots, up steep ridges and down.

"Who put this hill here?" Sally grumbled as we climbed another long grade. When we'd had the maps spread out on the floor back home, she must have overlooked the faint contour lines, each representing fifty feet of elevation gain. The trail crossed six lines at this portage.

When we stopped for a rest farther along the trail, I remarked that the map failed to show the more interesting features of the portage. Our clothes told a better story. Pant legs were coated with mud from a slope we had slid down, and moccasins were soaked with slimy water from a swamp crossing. Sally's shirtsleeve was torn by a sharp stick at a beaver dam we had scrambled over.

"A couple more times over this trail and we'll be in tatters!" Sally quipped.

Like the voyageurs, we had several loads of gear to portage. They had carried their burden for ten or fifteen minutes, then dropped it beside the trail and returned for another. When all the packs had been taken to one place, they were carried farther along the trail. Each place where the loads were put down was a *posé*. The portages came to be measured by the number of *posés* along the way.

For us, each portage involved one trip across with our canoe and three more trips each with packs. Including the return trips, the two-mile portage meant we had to walk the trail seven times, for a total of fourteen miles.

The voyageurs generally dogtrotted over the trail, leaning forward under the weight of two, and sometimes even three, ninety-pound loads.

"Ha! Three ninety-pound packs—sounds like a tall tale to me," I wheezed when we reached the end of a portage.

"Tighten up that sash, and you'll be good for another pack or two," Sally prodded. The colourful woven sash each of us wore around our waist was not merely for decoration; it also provided abdominal support. But despite the sashes, in days gone by hernias had been the leading cause of death after drowning.

Carrying our canoe voyageur-style

Our canoe laden with supplies for a month

Lugging our packs over the portages was a challenge, but carrying the canoe was even more difficult. We chose to carry our canoe in the same way the Northmen had carried theirs—right side up with one person at the bow and one at the stern. Sally and I stood in the water and braced ourselves to lift the weight.

We raised the canoe from the water to hip level, put our hands underneath the hull and heaved it to our shoulders. As I struggled up the hill from the lake, I didn't really mind the cooling stream of water that ran down my neck and back.

On our trips over with the packs, we had scouted the route in preparation for carrying the canoe. However, walking along a narrow, winding trail, while joined at the shoulders by a long canoe, took considerable planning and communication.

"Tree on the right," I warned at the first bend in the trail, giving Sally notice to swing wide. It was like getting a table through a doorway . . . twisting and sidestepping until we were past each tree. If we misjudged a corner, fingers or shoulders or canoe bark became bruised as they struck trees beside the trail.

Mosquitoes seem to have a special sense that tells them when their victims are helpless, as we were, with our hands unavailable for slapping as we carried the canoe. They buzzed, they bit. They tickled places we couldn't reach. Black flies were even more tormenting, flying under our cuffs and down our necks to feast on tender skin. Every bite drew blood, dotting our shirts with red.

"I need a break!" Sally's muffled call came from her end of the canoe.

"Doesn't look good," I reported. "I see only thick bush and rocks ahead."

With a groan, Sally shifted the canoe on her narrow shoulder and we continued plodding. Voyageurs had prided themselves in never letting their canoes touch the ground; we were not as particular, but didn't want to set ours down just anywhere. We needed a small clearing, level and free of sharp objects that could damage the bark.

"Can't go much farther!" Sally called out. We'd been staggering down the trail with the canoe on our shoulders for almost half an hour.

"I think there's a spot just around the corner," I replied. I'm sure Sally smiled at this age-old ploy of just one more bend or one more hill to our destination.

"Here's a good spot. Down on three," I said. Sally didn't even wait for my count of one. After a short rest, we gritted our teeth, heaved the canoe onto our shoulders, and continued along the trail.

It was the end of the day by the time we'd carried everything over the portage. Our arms ached and our backs were sore. My hair was plastered to my temples with sweat. As Sally had said along the way, the portage was a character-building experience.

Placing the last packs beside the others, we walked straight into the lake to cool off. Gradually, I became aware of something in the water with us. A beaver swam only three canoe-lengths away, nose above the water and two black eyes staring intently at the strange sight of Sally and me in the lake. The beaver slapped its tail on the water, only to resurface seconds later to study us again.

Mud from the trail was rinsed from our clothes as we swam, and the cool water soothed our muscles. We floated on our backs, savouring this simple pleasure.

"The good news is that from here the portages are shorter and our load gets lighter," Sally said as she wrung out her clothes. Then she plopped onto a log beside me. Although she said not a word, I began massaging her neck, knowing her muscles must be as sore as mine.

Voyageurs would never have let anyone know that their shoulders hurt, that they had blisters or sore muscles. Putting on a strong front was part of the bluster and bravado. One who complained or lagged behind would soon bear a nickname such as "grandpa" or "the turtle" or worse.

Sally and I were exhausted when we crawled into our tent that evening. For a few minutes I lay with eyes closed, listening to the sounds around us: the gentle soughing of wind in the treetops and the lapping of waves against the shore. Over the rustlings and swishings rose the insistent tap-tapping of a woodpecker. The echo sounded like a beak hammering on a hollow tree.

Suddenly, another possibility occurred to me. The canoe! Jolted by the thought, I sat up. Our canoe already bore the scars of a previous woodpecker's work, from when the bark was still on the tree. Now I had visions of another bird finishing the task.

I scrambled to the tent door. Peering into the low light, I was relieved to make out the dark shape of the woodpecker working on a nearby aspen. Once back in bed, I slept so soundly that even one of Tom's imaginary bears chewing on the canoe wouldn't have woken me.

The next morning we accompanied the call of loons with a chorus of "Frère Jacques," pulling hard on our paddles to the rhythm of the words. With Long Portage behind us, we were in high spirits.

Rose Lake, with rugged hills that rose abruptly from the shoreline, was even more beautiful than the lakes we had already paddled. The water was so clear we could watch the shadow of the canoe playing over boulders far beneath us. We took our time, canoeing close to shore in the cool shade of contrasting stands of pine and birch. The hardship of the last portage was forgotten as we listened to squirrels chattering and chickadees calling from within the forest. I filled my lungs with sweet-smelling, clean air, and revelled in the pristine wilderness around us.

Our high spirits were tempered only slightly when we had to paddle against the current of a narrow river flowing into the next lake.

"*C'est terrible,*" I called as we strained against the opposing current. To keep the flavour of the voyageur experience, we cursed, sang, and spoke French every now and then. Although Sally said my accent was atrocious, the meaning was usually evident.

Words failed me when the river narrowed to a point where the water was squeezed between two granite walls. White, foaming water surged towards us, splashing against dark rock. We stopped to survey the channel.

"What do you think? Can we paddle up the river?" Sally asked, hoping to avoid a portage. After studying the channel more closely, we decided that the river was too strong. A short carry and we were on South Lake.

Sally and I paddled briskly across the lake towards the one portage we actually looked forward to. After the Height of Land Portage, the rivers would flow in the direction we were headed—west and north, until we reached Lake Winnipeg.

At the end of the portage we paused, as all voyageurs had, for the traditional ceremony that took place here.

"Do you promise never to do anything that would bring dishonour to voyageurs?" Sally asked as she dipped a spruce bough in the clear water.

"*Oui,*" I answered, dropping to one knee in the sand.

"And never to kiss another voyageur's wife against her own free will?" she continued, sprinkling droplets of water over my head.

"*Oui.*"

"And never to let another man pass this way without taking the same oath?" she prodded.

When I answered yes to this question as well, she brushed my left shoulder, then right with the water-soaked spruce bough. Then I performed a similar ceremony for Sally. Years ago, the rite would have been concluded with a dozen gunshots and a treat of rum supplied by the newly initiated members.

Alexander Henry must have felt this ceremony was a thinly disguised excuse for a party when he wrote: "The voyageurs now expected all those on board to be treated with something to drink. Should a person refuse to comply, he would be sure of being plunged into the water, which they profanely call, baptizing him. To avoid such a disaster, I gave the people of my canoe a few bottles of spirits."

For the newly initiated voyageur, I suspect there was a deeper meaning to this ceremony than just the promise of a dram of liquor. This was the first step to becoming a Northman, an *homme du nord*. Those who spent winter in the North Country were due the respect of all voyageurs. And when they returned to Montreal after a year, or two, or three, it was their tales of grand adventure that lured young men to sign on. For all voyageurs, the ultimate goal was to be an *homme du nord*.

Sally and I drained a small flask we had carried for the occasion. This day was also special for us because it would bring the first rapids going our way. We paddled across North Lake with great anticipation. Would we be able to run the rapids marked on our map? Or would we have to carry our gear over another tedious portage?

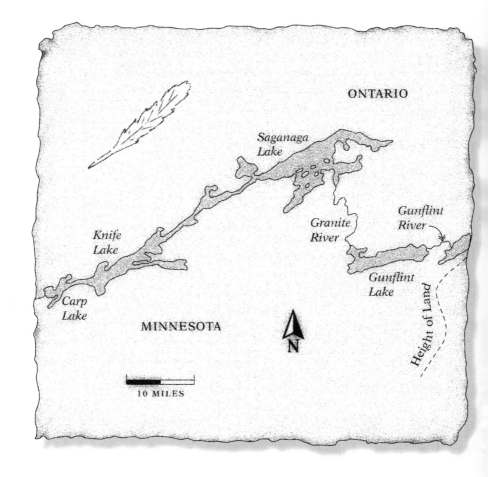

ONTARIO

Saganaga
Lake

Gunflint
River

Knife
Lake

Granite
River

Carp
Lake

Gunflint
Lake

MINNESOTA

N

Height of Land

10 MILES

FIVE

Canoe Country

Sally and I heard the roar of whitewater long before we came to the first rapids on the Gunflint River. Like distant thunder, the sound echoed between the low rock walls that bordered the waterway.

Backpaddling, we eased around the next bend, then saw the dancing white waves and tell-tale narrowing of the channel. Sally reached out with her paddle to steer the bow of the canoe into the safety of an eddy.

"I can't bear the thought of another portage now that the water is finally going our way!" Sally exclaimed.

We held the canoe off the rocks with our paddles and looked over the rapids. They started with a satin-slick flow of water between rocks, then led to a series of high, standing waves. I scanned the river for bulges of water that might indicate boulders just below the surface. Although we were eager to avoid a portage, we knew that a submerged rock could easily punch a hole in the bark hull of our canoe.

Sally and I climbed onto a rock and discussed our route through the rapids, planning the moves we would make. This would be our first run with the canoe in fast water. We both found reasons to delay our departure.

I rearranged the load in the canoe. Sally checked the knots on the bow and stern lines. Neither task was necessary, but they gave us some time to think about what lay ahead. I wondered how the loaded canoe would respond to our paddle strokes. Sally worried that we might have difficulty steering around the midstream boulder. We both questioned if the lashings holding the canoe together would come loose as it flexed in the turbulent water.

"Well?" Sally asked.

"Okay . . . let's go for it!" I answered, climbing back into the canoe.

I wrapped my fingers tightly around my paddle and took a deep breath.

"*Allez!*" I called, and Sally thrust her paddle into the water, pulling the bow into the current. White waves splashed over the canoe as we sped down the river.

"Rock on the right!" Sally yelled.

Even though we steered hard left, the canoe banged against the rock. The heavily laden canoe was slower to respond and more difficult to steer than we had expected.

"Left!"

"Right!"

"Backpaddle!" We shouted instructions back and forth as the river surged around us.

Sally called something to me, but her voice was overpowered by the sound of rushing water. She leaned out and thrust her paddle into the river to pull the canoe away from another rock. In the time it took me to counteract her movement, we tipped sideways.

Water surged over the gunwale. I leaned hard the other way, righting the canoe.

As we straightened the canoe, a wave lifted the bow skyward, then dropped us into a deep trough with a splash that drenched Sally. The entire canoe shuddered, flexing with the impact.

Ankle-deep water sloshed around my feet as we hurtled down the river. With the extra weight of the water, the canoe became even more difficult to control. Backpaddling furiously, we narrowly missed another rock.

Sally pulled hard on her paddle to turn the canoe. Left, right, and left. I heard a loud *crack!* as her paddle struck a submerged rock, almost knocking it out of her hands. I fought to keep the canoe straight in the current. Finally we pulled ashore in calmer water.

"Needs work," Sally remarked, laughing as we stood beside the canoe.

"Well, just a little," I responded, putting my arm around my very wet partner and pulling her close to me. She tipped her head sideways, and water that had pooled in the brim of her soggy straw hat sluiced down my neck. Somehow, the romantic mood was broken.

As we bailed out the canoe, we talked about what we would do differently at the next rapids.

"The canoe is a lot heavier than we're used to," I said. "If you give each boulder a wider berth, I'll have time to follow your moves."

"Okay, and I could start my turns a bit earlier to give us more room to manoeuvre," Sally responded. For the rest of the fast water we practised our river-running techniques. Then the river widened and we were flushed into the next lake.

Canoeing the length of Gunflint Lake was slow-paced and relaxing after the adrenaline-pumping stretches of white-water. Cruising along the lakeshore, we had time to absorb the aura of the wilderness around us. Emerald green water mirrored the reflections of rugged pine trees and rocky escarpments. What struck us most was the silence: no voices, no hum of civilization, just the occasional lonesome call of a loon. We felt a sense of well-being that comes to us only in wild places.

Under the hot summer sun, we paddled steadily. I came to appreciate the design of our old-style shirts, with the broad shoulders that allowed ease of movement and kept us cool. Even so, we stopped now and then to have a refreshing dip in the lake and to rinse the sweat from our shirts.

A day later, with the lake behind us, another series of rapids beckoned as the Granite River wound through bedrock channels. We pulled into an eddy to survey the river.

Years ago, voyageurs might have pulled into this same eddy and waited while the guide in charge surveyed the rapids. To the guide, a stretch of whitewater would be an old friend . . . or perhaps an enemy. He would have come to know it over the years as he had risen in the ranks from a young, inexperienced paddler. He would know that a set of rapids that was safe in one season could be deadly in another; high water caused a faster current, while low water exposed dangerous rocks. His decision would determine whether the paddlers ran the fast water or had to portage.

"This looks like a *demi-charge*," Sally said after we had studied the rapids. I agreed. We would remove half our load to lighten the canoe and make it easier to handle.

The course down shallow rapids is often through the biggest waves where the water is deepest. The guide would have decided whether the crew was to paddle faster than the current or backpaddle to slow the canoe. Either choice would give the steersman the ability to manoeuvre the canoe through the rapids.

"I think we should backpaddle," I suggested. The river was moving through the narrows in a blur, and I had no desire to paddle faster than that!

Kneeling to keep our centre of gravity low, we started down the rapids. I could see Sally's shoulders tense as she concentrated on the river. With a shout and some deft paddle work by Sally, we blasted through the first standing wave.

The next wave splashed over Sally, dampening her enthusiasm somewhat. Then, as suddenly as it had started, the ride was over. The current spat us into calm water.

"I was planning to wash my shirt anyway," Sally declared as she wrung out her sodden clothes and poured water from her moccasins. I sponged out the water that had

Running the rapids

Tumping a load past impassable rapids

flowed to the low end of the canoe. Although we had taken on some water, Sally and I were pleased with our progress in guiding the canoe.

"Ready to line the canoe back upriver for another load?" I asked, reminding Sally that voyageurs often hauled an empty canoe back upriver to the starting point to pick up the half-load they had left behind.

"Sure . . . if we trade places," she replied, knowing that I preferred to paddle in the stern. After a short discussion of the merits of running the river solo, I agreed that one trip down this wild stretch of water was enough. Hoping that no ghosts of voyageurs were frowning with disapproval, we walked along the portage trail to retrieve our other packs.

In 1800, Alexander Henry had written of the perils of running rapids: "One of my canoes, to avoid the trouble of making the portage, passed down near the N. shore with a full load. She had not gone many yards when, by some mismanagement of the foreman, the current bore down her bow full upon the shore, against a rock, whilst the current whirled the canoe around. The canoe was instantly carried out and lost to view amongst the high waves. At length, she appeared and stood perpendicular for a moment, when she sank down again." The cargo, canoe, and one voyageur were lost in the maelstrom.

With that in mind, we portaged our canoe and packs around the next rapids. In travelling through this wild country, we had to take responsibility for our actions and the consequences. This applied to every decision we made, from running rapids to crossing exposed bays on the lakes.

At each set of rapids, we took into account our canoeing abilities, the way our canoe handled in moving water, and the added consideration of paddling an easily damaged birchbark craft. Even so, we knew there was always a chance that something could happen. Risks are part of adventure. Our goal was to minimize the risks.

Two more portages and one *décharge* later, where we ran a set of rapids with an empty canoe, we reached Saganaga Lake. The lake featured an extravagance of islands, some topped with gnarled pine trees, others just barren slabs of rock. The shoreline was primitive and wild, with fissured granite, thick with clinging mosses and ferns. Winding our way from island to island, we paddled along the south shore of the largest body of water we had encountered so far.

Now, a week from Grand Portage, our life had taken on the rhythm of wilderness travel. On the lakes our pace slowed. Each time we came to rapids our paddling tempo increased, reflecting the energy of the river.

Each morning, we rose at dawn. Then, fuelled by tea, we began paddling. Breakfast would come later—perhaps during a shore break, or more likely during a rest stop on the water, with *galette* passed between us on a paddle.

Like the voyageurs before us, we stopped every hour or so for a rest. From pouches hung on their sashes, the paddlers would have pulled out tobacco for a *pipe*, a smoke break. Lakes were measured not in miles or leagues, but in *pipes*, with each one representing approximately one hour of travel, depending on wind and waves.

Pipes were sometimes taken on land, although a rest stop in the canoe had the advantage of fewer mosquitoes to torment the men. The voyageurs would lay their paddles across the gunwales and let their canoes drift. Occasionally, they might have tied up to a small, bug-free island so they could stretch legs that had been wedged between bundles for many hours.

For voyageurs, Saganaga Lake would have been four *pipes* long. Although Sally and I don't smoke, this means of measuring progress fit well with our view of long-distance paddling. We rarely thought in terms of distance, but in time; time between rest stops, time to each *posé* on a portage trail, and time to travel the length of a lake. On a larger scale, our goal was to reach our first resupply point by the end of our third week of paddling.

Part way down peaceful Saganaga Lake, Sally suddenly burst into song, a version of "Alouette" loud enough to lift a flock of geese off the water.

"*Alouette, gentille alouette. Alouette, je t'y plumerai,*" she sang. I couldn't tell whether the flock had scattered because she was singing about plucking birds, or whether they objected to the sheer volume.

"Je t'y plumerai la tête, je t'y plumerai la tête. Et la tête, et la tête! Alouette, alouette!"

As the last words of the song echoed off the granite hills, Sally turned and grinned at me over her shoulder.

"We need something to focus on other than the scorching sun or the long lake," she said. "It's my job to whip our spirits up. As I recall, the voyageurs did this through song . . . "

"Not drink?" I suggested hopefully.

"Song!" Sally remained firm. And so, when she launched into another French folk song, I joined her. I didn't remind her that it had been the voyageur in the stern who initiated the songs when the pace of the paddles began to slow.

Singing helped us keep the rhythm of forty strokes per minute. Voyageurs had often paddled at an even faster cadence. It was staggering to think that a long day on the lakes might have involved lifting a paddle more than forty thousand times! The men had sung of canoes, the country, life, loves, church . . . and off-colour versions of old and new songs. Singing lustily did make the time go faster, I had to admit.

Even though Sally had grown up in Quebec and had a fair repertoire of French songs, we still felt the tedium of paddling hour after hour. For variety, we canoed close to shore where we could listen to a medley of birdsong, watch the occasional weasel bound along the rocks, or just enjoy paddling in the shade of the mixed forest.

Along the way, we searched openings in the forest for the tell-tale green carpet of bushes that might offer a bounty of blueberries. They were always a good reason for a shore break. With bow and stern ropes of the canoe each tied to a boulder, we would anchor the canoe in shallow water. Then we picked blueberries until our fingers and tongues were purple. If there were enough berries, we might even save some for dessert that evening.

Paddling close to shore also gave us an opportunity to look for tracks in sandy coves. A neat row of dog-like tracks showed where a fox had come to the water. Farther on, webbed prints told a story of a beaver that had wandered onto shore to cut down a tree. A long trough in the sand indicated where the beaver had dragged the tree to the lake, and a profusion of tracks and wood chips told of an evening meal at the water's edge.

Not all tracks were pleasing to the eye. One evening as a storm was brewing, we approached a beach that looked like an ideal place to camp. While I stood in the water holding the canoe, Sally scouted out the potential campsite. She hesitated at the shore.

"Bear tracks!" she called, pointing to fresh tracks that led out of the woods and across the beach. Each print was as long as Sally's moccasin. With a sigh, Sally waded back to the canoe and climbed in. Although we had been paddling for ten hours already, we continued down the lake.

In the distance, towering thunderheads rumbled ominously. A black curtain of rain joined lake and cloud. Aware of the brooding power of the storm, we paddled faster, anxious to get off the water.

I could feel the cold breath of the storm down the back of my neck when we spied another sheltered cove. It featured all we needed for a good campsite: a level area for the tent and plenty of driftwood for a fire. Best of all, there were no bear tracks. I quickly unloaded the packs and stacked our gear on the beach.

As the first patter of rain dimpled the surface of the water, we carried the canoe to shore. We tucked it in the shelter of the forest, safe from the winds that could pick it up and send it tumbling across the beach.

With practised speed, we set up the canvas tent, diving in just before the skies opened. There is an elemental pleasure in beating a storm, and we revelled in the relative warmth and comfort of the tent. Snug beneath our trade blankets, we listened to the raindrops drumming against canvas. Brilliant flashes of light illuminated the tent, followed by

A rest stop along the way

Cooking pea soup

thunder that shook the earth beneath us. The musty smell of damp soil permeated the air.

The storm passed just as the canvas started to drip where my elbow had pressed against the side of the tent. We scrambled outside, and began to prepare supper before the next shower.

For a special treat, I cooked up a concoction called rubbaboo. I threw a handful of flour into a pot of boiling water, then added several chunks of pemmican. After simmering over the fire for a while, the result was a brown, greasy soup. A few twigs, a swarm of mosquitoes, and dirt from a stick used for stirring would have made it an even more authentic dish.

Like voyageurs years ago, we sat around the campfire, each dipping into the pot with a mug.

"Mmmm. Tastes like grease, flour, and water," Sally said tactfully.

"That's probably because it is. Glad you like it!" I replied.

Later that evening, Sally leaned against me, sipping hot tea from her tin mug. Her face was bronzed from days of sun and wind, her hands were calloused from gripping a paddle, and her calico shirt was beginning to look faded and trail-worn.

"This voyageur life suits me just fine," she said. "Funny how a hearty meal erases the memory of difficult portages and long days of paddling."

The next morning brought another portage only an hour from camp. Even though our packs were cumbersome and the trail was rough, we didn't really mind. The portage provided a change of pace from paddling. It was an opportunity for time alone after days of travelling only two paddle-lengths apart. I walked at my own pace, lost in thought.

Looking at the forest around me, I noted several birch trees with suitable bark for repairing a canoe. Jack pine on the hill I'd just climbed or spruce in the last swampy area could supply roots for lashings. I was truly becoming a voyageur, right down to scanning the forest for materials to repair our canoe.

Back on the river, I realized that we had become one with the canoe, instinctively reacting to each situation we encountered. River canoeing is part intuition and part action; what we had learned at each stretch of whitewater helped us paddle the next.

Now, we moved through the fast water with an economy of paddle strokes. With few words spoken, we worked as a team and manoeuvred confidently through the boulder garden.

"Remember the first rapids?" Sally said laughing when we pulled out for a rest.

"Yeah, I kind of miss the thrill of wondering when we'll tip!" I replied. A splash from her paddle told me she didn't totally agree.

My wish for some excitement came just downriver when the water poured through a chasm with speed enough to potentially crush our canoe and scatter our gear. As we pulled to shore I looked up to the hilltop, half expecting to see the crosses of centuries ago, still bearing the names of voyageurs who had perished here.

There were no crosses, but this undoubtedly would have been the location of many. A trader long ago had written of a place such as this in his journal: "During the day, we have come upon several difficult rapids, where many persons have drowned, either in coming up or going down. For every such unfortunate person, whether his corpse is found or not, a cross is erected by his companions. At this place, I see no less than fourteen."

Even so, I could understand why voyageurs ran dubious-looking rapids. Sally and I were not eager to make another portage, and the fast-moving water tempted us to take the risk, to run the channel.

Paddle, paddle, paddle, the river seemed to murmur as it coursed fluidly between dark rocks. I looked at the whitewater again. The constant movement of water was mesmerizing.

"I think we could canoe this, after all," I said, gazing longingly at the river.

"And I think no voyageur ever drowned on a portage," Sally replied. Then she picked up a pack and began walking down the trail. Without the group bravado that existed among the voyageurs, it was easier to keep our resolve to be cautious.

By late afternoon, we reached Knife Lake, named for the sharp pieces of slate that extend along the shoreline and over the portage trails. As we set up camp, we left the canoe upside down to dry in the sun. After the last portage we had noticed water trickling in. I had been sponging out the canoe frequently as we paddled up the lake; it was time to regum the seams.

"Here's one leak," Sally said, pointing to where a rock had rubbed off the gum. I found another leak where a seam had opened slightly.

Retrieving a glowing stick from the fire, I used it to dribble spruce gum onto the seam. Travelling had put a lot of strain on the canoe. At each set of rapids, the bark yielded to the force of the raging water. Now and then, the canoe had bumped against an unseen boulder under the water. In some ways, the portages had been just as hard on the canoe. The hot summer sun softened the gum, and the hull flexed each time we had lifted the canoe or wrestled it around a tight turn on the trail.

As we regummed the canoe, we also inspected the bark for damage. Earlier in the day we had run a stretch of whitewater and misjudged the width of the canoe, bouncing off a half-submerged rock. A new crease ran along the right side of the hull.

"By the end of the trip, each scrape and each bruise will tell a story," Sally said, reflecting on our river-running escapades.

"And I bet the stories that make the greatest impressions will be at your end of the canoe," I added.

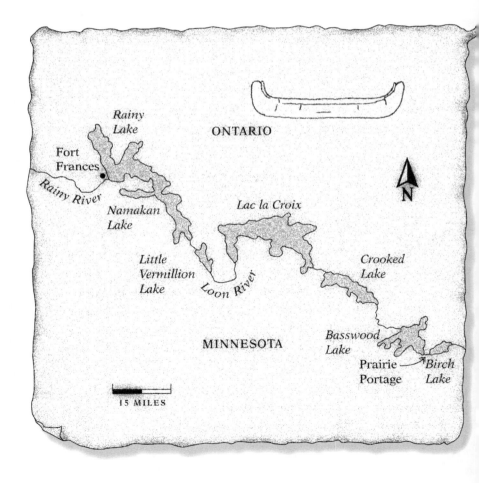

Rainy Lake

ONTARIO

Fort Frances

Rainy River

Namakan Lake

Lac la Croix

Little Vermillion Lake

Loon River

Crooked Lake

MINNESOTA

Basswood Lake

Prairie Portage

Birch Lake

N

15 MILES

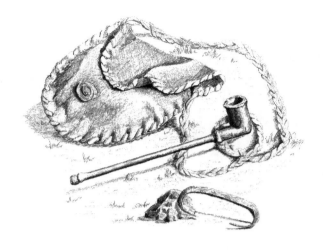

SIX

Voyageur Life

As Sally and I approached Prairie Portage, we saw eight canoes vying for a good landing place at the trailhead. People scurried back and forth, unloading cargo and carrying packs to shore.

After the solitude of the past two weeks, we were dismayed by the noise and confusion. Then it occurred to us how similar this scene was to the days when voyageurs had arrived at a portage. As in the past, packs from many canoes were strewn on the shore, at risk of being mixed up. We heard the grunts and groans of paddlers struggling with their loads along the portage trail. And we felt the age-old competition to get to the next lake and beat others to the best launching sites.

Mostly, we felt excitement in anticipation of a planned rendezvous with two friends from Vancouver. Months ago, they had arranged to accompany us for the next week of our journey. After lugging our gear and canoe across the portage, we looked over to a small island.

"Do you think they'll be there?" I asked as we scanned the shoreline. Sally was first to spot the column of smoke from a campfire. Hoping that it was not other campers, we eagerly paddled over. A volley of pine cones lobbed from the shore confirmed it was our friends.

"Christophe! Laurent!" Sally called, using French versions of their names.

That evening, while feasting on fresh meat and vegetables, we shared stories of our journey. By the time we had finished the wine Chris and Laurie had brought, my tales had become somewhat embellished. Our feats would have impressed any voyageur.

"Seems to me that if you were so fast and so strong, you would have been here sooner," Chris interjected.

"Ah, but our load is also extraordinary," I replied.

"Speaking of loads, we're pleased to help lighten yours before the journey," Sally added, reaching for another piece of the chocolate dessert. For some reason, they refused my offer to trade our lightweight pemmican for their heavy cans of corned beef.

"You'll be sorry when we come to the first portage," I taunted, pulling out maps of our route. Beside the campfire, we looked over the maps and traced the blue line of waterways we would follow for the next week. Like most novice voyageurs, Chris and Laurie had some reservations about what lay ahead. They were not accustomed to canoeing long distances or packing heavy loads. However, like the young farm-hands of centuries ago, stories of adventure and beautiful scenery had lured them from the comforts of home.

Chris and Laurie's first day of travel did little to put them at ease. We canoed along the south shore of Basswood Lake, threading our way through a maze of channels and islands, while Sally used an old-style brass compass for navigation.

"Are we lost yet?" Chris asked, when we stopped to check the map for the fifth time in an hour. I wondered how guides could possibly have found their way through all the turns and twists of this difficult passage. Then I remembered they had marked their route with "lob sticks."

A lob stick had been made by selecting a tall pine on a

prominent point or island. One of the voyageurs would have volunteered to climb the tree, axe tucked in his sash, and cut away all but a few top branches. The conspicuous tree then served as a landmark for future paddlers.

Even without lob sticks, we managed to find our way onto the open water of Basswood Lake. Six hours of paddling later, Chris begged to stop for the night.

"My arms are going to fall off!" he protested wearily. Chris and Laurie headed for their tent right after supper, exhausted from the first day of paddling.

Their second day was not much easier. It began with an arduous one-mile portage around Upper Basswood Falls. As Chris and Laurie struggled over the trail, I wasn't sure they fully appreciated the beauty of the falls. But as I passed Laurie, he held his arm out to stop me.

"I've never seen anything like it," he wheezed. Laurie was so awestruck, he'd forgotten about the heavy pack on his back. We stood together for a few minutes, gazing at the thundering green walls of water that poured over an outcrop of granite. A vivid rainbow arched overhead, disappearing and reappearing in the mist from the falls. At the edge of the cascade, a winding trail dropped almost as abruptly as the water, over steep, broken rock.

On my way back from a trip over the portage trail, I found Chris sprawled beside the trail, staring at his heavy pack.

"*Eh, monsieur,* camping for the night?" I taunted. His answer, in gasps, questioned the sanity of a person subjecting themselves to such torture.

When I returned to our packs at the lake, I thought of the tricks that would have been played on new crew members. One had been to hide rocks in a pack and watch the novice struggle over the portage with a load that seemed much too heavy. That method of initiating Chris and Laurie appealed to me, but they had the chocolate bars. The thought of jeopardizing this source of nutrition held me back.

Nevertheless, it was customary to play a trick on the newcomers. So, at the end of the portage, I hid their spare paddle under our load and watched as they searched for it among their gear. Disgust showed on their faces when they thought of having to walk all the way back for such a small thing.

I let them search for several minutes, listening to: "I thought you brought it," and "I'm sure I did," until I finally produced the paddle.

"We owe you one," Laurie said, heaving a sigh of relief.

Less than an hour later, our canoes entered a marshy bay where mud-flats extended far from shore. We paddled until the canoes became stuck in the mud. Then, knee-deep in black ooze, we stumbled over unseen roots and rocks, struggling to reach dry ground.

"Are we having fun yet?" Chris asked. No one replied. Wading through the slough of decaying vegetation, bird droppings, and stagnant water would have discouraged even the most hardy voyageur. I pitied the one chosen to cross this stretch of muck with a *bourgeois* on his back.

Our third portage of the day ended at a steep, thirty-foot drop to the water. Step by step, boulder by boulder, we struggled to carry the canoes down the cliff. Then, passing heavy packs from hand to hand, we loaded the canoes.

After two weeks on the trail, Sally and I were inured to the grind of the portages. Even so, we had to admit that this had been one of our tougher days. By the time we stopped for the night, Chris and Laurie were dead tired. Still, we found enough energy to banter back and forth, comparing prowess on the portages and skills at the campsite.

"You're like lightning with that axe, Ian," Chris taunted as I chopped wood for the fire. "You never strike the same place twice!"

That led to comments about their performance on the portage trail. Almost inevitably, the evening ended with boasts of the qualities of our respective canoes. Ours was admittedly heavier on the portages, but we praised its stability in rough water. Chris pointed out how light their canoe was, adding that the narrow profile meant it would be faster on the lakes.

Paddling past cliffs in Quetico Park

Hauling packs over a beaver dam

A couple of days later, we had an opportunity to see how their canoe measured up in whitewater. We arrived at a roiling set of rapids and stopped just upriver to check them out. The rarely used portage trail was rough and rocky, ascending a cliff and then leading along a precariously narrow ledge above the river. We went ashore to discuss the best route down the rapids. Chris and Laurie were uncharacteristically quiet.

"How about watching us, then following our route?" Sally suggested. Chris nodded slowly, then cast another glance at the rapids.

Sally and I climbed into our canoe, paddled to mid-river, then headed directly towards the chute. Just before the first standing wave, Sally drew the bow to the left. A quick backstroke . . . then a twist of my paddle and we pivoted around a black boulder. We straightened out and side-slipped to the right. Then we shot the last chute and turned abruptly into an eddy at the base of the rapids.

"Let's not mention how many rapids we ran before learning how to handle this canoe," I said to Sally. She laughed and held her paddle in the air in triumph.

From the eddy, we watched Chris and Laurie linger at the river's edge for the longest time. Finally, they climbed into their canoe. They brought the canoe to the lip of the chute, backpaddling furiously.

Their manoeuvres were not as well timed as ours. They had just started down the chute when their canoe hit an underwater rock, tipped precariously, and then ricocheted off another boulder. Then they hit the black boulder head-on. The canoe bounced out of the water as Chris held onto the gunwales with both hands. The last thing we saw was a blur of yellow as their canoe shot past the eddy and continued downriver.

We finally caught up with them around the next bend.

"Lucky you're in a fibreglass boat. A birchbark canoe would have been kindling after that," Sally said.

"Hey, you have your style, we have ours," Laurie said, grinning from ear to ear.

When we reached the next stretch of whitewater, Chris and Laurie were eager to continue. But as I looked downriver, I saw a crest of water that indicated a submerged rock part way through the rapids. Just to the right, in the only clear passage, an innocent-looking swell meant another rock lurked there as well.

"Are you sure you want to tackle this one?" I asked.

To sway their decision, I read what Alexander Henry had said about his crew: "The canoemen had not gone far, when to avoid the ridge of waves, they took the apparent smooth water and were drawn into a whirlpool, which wheeled them around into its vortex. The Canoe with the Men clinging to it, went down end foremost."

"That would be us," Chris said. His newly acquired tan had faded somewhat and his knuckles were white where he gripped his paddle. "I guess we'll portage."

"Great pep talk, Ian. That story even convinced *me* to walk," Sally added.

Two other canoeists were just ahead of us on the portage, and when we finished our last carry, Sally noticed one of our packs was missing. After a hasty but thorough search, I began to worry as I thought of all the essentials in the missing pack.

"The other guys must have taken it by mistake," I said grumpily. "We'll have to paddle hard to catch up to them!"

"Chris and I will just sit here and munch on some chocolate while you two chase them," Laurie said, settling onto a sun-warmed boulder. There was a touch of mischief in his voice, and I studied him suspiciously. They burst into laughter.

"*Monsieur,* the pack you are looking for is back up the trail . . . at the top of the long hill."

I groaned. This was his retaliation for the trick I had played on them. I trudged up the steep hill, searching for the pack in the bushes. Five minutes later, I realized I had been duped! Why would Laurie have lugged the heavy pack up the hill? I hiked back, and there it was, in its rightful place among our gear.

The next day, I noticed that Chris and Laurie seemed unusually reluctant to leave their gear unattended.

"You are developing the protective instincts of true voyageurs," I congratulated my friends. "But they would have been watching out for marauding competitors, not their own crew." I tried to look wounded, but they laughed.

We continued north towards Lac la Croix, taking turns leading and sometimes taking shortcuts to get ahead of the other canoe. As the channel narrowed, sheer cliffs rose abruptly from the water's edge, towering a hundred feet above us. The fissured face of each cliff, coloured with orange, black, and pale-green lichens, was reflected in the shimmering depths below. Now, paddling in the shadow of the high cliffs, we spoke in hushed tones, awed by the grandeur of the rocky shore.

When we reached the open water of Lac la Croix, the wind started to build. Sally cautioned the others to follow the shoreline. By afternoon, wind was howling across the lake and whitecaps topped the cresting waves. I felt the same responsibility that a guide from the days of the fur trade would have. To wait here would mean lost time on our tight schedule. To paddle into the wind could expose us to waves that could swamp a canoe. It was a difficult decision. Although a guide would have made his decision alone, we put it to a vote.

"Let's go for it," Chris said, impatient to be travelling.

"Are you sure you want to, in that low-sided craft you call a canoe?" I questioned. Laurie was as eager to paddle as Chris, so we agreed to forge ahead.

Paddling into the wind and waves was slow and tedious, but not too difficult until we rounded a point that had served as a breakwater. Now we paddled straight into the full force of the storm. It became obvious that Chris and Laurie had never been in big waves before—and this was a poor place to teach them how to handle a canoe in open water.

"Point the bow just off the waves, towards shore," I called to them as the canoes bucked in the surf. Sally held our bow into the waves while I watched the others.

Chris and Laurie were both grim-faced, white-knuckled, and paddling hard. Our canoe rode the waves more easily, but even Sally and I felt uncomfortable on the open water. It was now impossible for Chris and Laurie to turn around and head back; to do so would have brought their canoe broadside to the waves. I could think of only one way out.

I urged Sally to paddle as close as possible to their canoe, and just ahead of them. With our canoe positioned at a slight angle, we absorbed the shock of each oncoming wave. This protected their boat from the brunt of the storm.

"Drift backwards," I called. "Keep your bow into the waves and let them push you back around the point!" This logic appealed to their sense of survival, and they stopped paddling. Fifteen minutes later, we were in smaller waves and they felt confident enough to turn into a protected cove.

After unloading the canoes, we tucked our tents into the shelter of trees to wait out the storm. A campfire dried wave-soaked clothes, and mugs of hot chocolate cheered four soggy paddlers. Every now and then one of us would get up to look at the waves, report on their size, and wonder when it would be safe to paddle again.

Just before sunset, I stood at the shore, leaning into the wind. The lake was a wild, hauntingly beautiful scene of crashing surf, dark scudding clouds, and trees bent from the force of the wind. In the distance, the last rays of the setting sun cast beams of crimson between clouds and the horizon.

Later that evening I played "Frère Jacques" on a tin whistle for entertainment, then produced my jaw harp and twanged a couple of off-key tunes.

"I hope you're not going to serenade us through the night," Chris said as they headed to their tent.

"No, but I'll give a performance at four in the morning if the wind has dropped," I replied.

The storm did ease somewhat by dawn. Although the lake was still strewn with waves, it looked tame compared to the

Playing the tin whistle

Early morning in camp

scene the previous day. With renewed enthusiasm, Chris and Laurie paddled into the waves as we continued along Lac la Croix.

By late afternoon we reached the Loon River. Floating lazily with the current, we passed bays thick with marsh grass and bulrushes. We paused to watch a cow moose and calf in a quiet backwater. The cow's ears twitched back and forth as she detected our presence. Then, with strings of lilies dangling from her mouth, she high-stepped through the water and into the forest with her calf close behind.

Around the next bend, we paddled through a mass of giant green lily pads. The slow pace of the river offered a pleasant change from wild rapids and windswept lakes. Even the portages were benign compared to the gut-busting climbs of the past days.

As we carried our packs over a portage, I was pleased to see that our paddling companions were becoming more accustomed to the long days of travel. By the time we reached Little Vermilion Lake two days later, Chris and Laurie were keeping pace with our canoe. They put on a spurt of speed and pulled up beside us.

"Hey, you call yourselves voyageurs? You paddle like my grandmother!" Laurie shouted as their bow came in line with ours.

"And you, with the big voice and small paddle, you paddle like my three-year-old nephew!" came Sally's response.

"Last crew to the point makes the fire tonight!"

No other words were spoken, nor would they have been two hundred years ago. In response, our strokes increased from forty per minute, to fifty, then fifty-five, and more. The canoes surged ahead.

Stiffening our arms and curving our backs, Sally and I pulled our red blades through the water. We strained against the paddles. Even so, Chris and Laurie edged ahead of us. Theirs was a faster canoe, but we were stronger—the odds were about even.

The bow of each canoe cleaved the surface of the lake, sending water gurgling back to paddles that slashed, then swirled the liquid aside. The wake from Chris and Laurie's canoe crept steadily forward along the side of our craft.

"Faster! Faster!" I urged Sally, and we increased our paddling speed. One stroke per second, sixty per minute, we churned the water into a froth.

"Change," Sally called, and we alternated sides without missing a beat. The miles and years we had paddled together were to our advantage. Slowly, our broad-beamed canoe gained on theirs.

"Maybe you should take the anchor up, *messieurs,*" Sally taunted as we edged past them. We arrived at the point only one canoe-length in the lead. Hearts pounded, sweat dripped from brows. Words came in short gasps. We drifted for a while, each catching our breath, with hardly enough lung-power for the usual banter between canoes.

That evening as we sat around the campfire, Sally entertained the crew with stories of wild rapids we had run and narrow escapes from the jaws of icy rivers. Then I told my most frightening bear story, from a trip several years earlier, of a bear that had charged down a river bank and chased us through shallow water. Our paddles had thrashed the water to a white foam as we pulled away from the charging bear.

My story contained vivid descriptions of the bear's flashing fangs, the sound of claws cleaving the air beside me, and the hot fishy smell of the beast's breath. I finished with the statement that the force of the spray from our paddles must have temporarily blinded the beast. Whatever the reason, the bear had stopped pursuing us and we escaped unscathed.

"You didn't jump out and wrestle the bear to submission?" Chris asked.

"That would be stretching the truth," I replied.

After a few more stories, Sally and I offered to cook a voyageur meal for our last evening together. While I cooked up a pot of pea soup, Sally began to make *galette*. She opened our canvas flour-bag and made a small hollow, then poured in a scoop of lake water. With bare hands, she mixed the dough in the bag, then kneaded it into a flat cake. Finally, she placed it on a hot rock beside the fire to cook.

"Where's that tot of rum you said voyageurs got each evening?" Chris asked as we ate supper.

"You have to earn it by leaping over the campfire," I replied. I went on to tell them that the contest usually involved building the flames higher and higher until only the bravest dared jump over it.

"I've had enough tests today," Laurie replied, rubbing his sore shoulder muscles.

"And you, Chris?"

"After you," he replied, waving a hand gallantly towards the blazing campfire. It was just as well they declined . . . I didn't care to risk burning my tender parts over a campfire either.

"Ah well, you have already proven yourselves as voyageurs," I conceded.

Our conversation turned to the tests that Chris and Laurie had passed on their journey. After warming up to the topic, I presented Chris and Laurie with birchbark certificates describing their accomplishments in my best calligraphy. Each was embellished with a sketch of crossed canoe paddles. With great ceremony, I unrolled a scroll and read the words.

"Let all mortals know that this person has passed the eight tests of a canoeman. He has completed a gruelling one-mile portage; run raging rapids in fine style; paddled into a gale-force wind; found a hidden portage trail; endured clouds of hungry mosquitoes; braved thunderstorms and torrential rain; unloaded a canoe in knee-deep mud; and paddled across wave-swept Lac la Croix. He is now a *Voyageur*. Quetico, Ontario. July 25th, 1998."

"I don't know what to say," Chris began, looking touched as I handed him his birchbark scroll.

"Say you'll be up first to light the fire tomorrow," Sally suggested. That idea spurred Sally to share one last voyageur tale before we went to our tents.

"You know, years ago, the tent poles had been placed in

the bottom of the canoes to keep the loads dry. If the occupants of a tent were not up soon enough, the other voyageurs would take great delight in collapsing the tent so the canoes could be loaded."

Chris and Laurie must have taken note, for they were up bright and early the next morning. We ate our last breakfast together. Then we loaded our canoes, each checking for boulders that might have been added to our packs in the night.

"*Bon voyage,*" Chris called, as they pointed their canoe south to their take-out point on Crane Lake.

Sally and I held our paddles high in a voyageur-style salute, then turned our canoe and headed north.

SEVEN

To the Rendezvous!

As our canoe slipped through the shadowed corridor of Namakan Narrows, we saw the marks of ancient glaciers etched into the granite walls. It was pleasantly cool, with deep, green water beneath our canoe and cliffs high above.

A thousand paddle strokes later, we glided from shadow to sunlight, onto Namakan Lake. Sally and I each lay our paddles across the gunwales and gazed at the scene before us. Emerald green water sparkled in the sun, contrasting with sloping sheets of pink granite that bordered the lake. Gnarled, weather-worn pine trees clung tenaciously to the rock.

I thought of how little this land had changed since the days when voyageurs plied these waters. The scene was starkly beautiful. And the barren shore was as devoid of suitable tent sites as it had been for voyageurs.

By late afternoon, we began scouting for a place to camp.

"How about over there?" Sally asked, pointing with her paddle to a boulder-strewn beach.

"Too rocky!"

In the next bay, Sally tried again.

"There's a level spot," she said.

"Too close to the water!" I replied, visualizing waves sloshing into the tent if the wind came up.

As the sun neared the horizon, Sally pointed out another site. It was an almost-level slab of granite, several paces from the water's edge. When I hesitated, she made it fairly clear that I could sleep there or in the canoe.

There is an art to setting up a canvas tent on bare rock— one we hadn't quite mastered. Perched tenuously on the smooth rock, we tied one rope of our tent to the overturned canoe and another to a stunted pine. Unable to anchor the tent with pegs, we piled boulders on each corner.

"Comfy?" Sally asked as we snuggled under a blanket in the tent. The rock beneath us was as cold as the glacier that had once passed over it.

Groaning, I adjusted my body to fit the contours of the hard surface under me, padding the lump between my shoulders with my shirt and ignoring another bump in the small of my back. A bed of marsh grass or spruce boughs like the voyageurs had used might have helped, but the rocky shoreline offered neither.

The next morning we were up before sunrise, sipping tea and massaging sore hips and shoulders.

"I remember one of the fur traders writing that a day of hard labour will enable a person to sleep as soundly on the ground as a sluggard will sleep on a bed of down," Sally said, warming her hands on her mug.

"Maybe," I acknowledged, rolling my stiff neck. "But there's a big difference between 'ground' and a slab of glacier-etched granite." Like two aged voyageurs, we walked stiffly around camp, creaking and groaning when we bent over to roll up the tent.

An hour of canoeing, however, chased the kinks out of our bodies. We settled into the steady rhythm of our all-day paddling speed. The sun warmed our backs. A loon called from across the lake. All was well in our world.

Three more days of paddling and three more nights of sleeping on rock brought us to our last portage before Rainy Lake.

"Thirty-six down . . . only twelve more to Cumberland House!" I said, dropping my pack at the end of the portage. From here, the lakes and rivers would be longer and the portages much shorter.

Three days later, just as we neared the west end of Rainy Lake, a storm blew across the open water. We paddled down a channel towards Black Bay to find shelter from the wind and waves. There, like a mirage on the water, lay two North canoes. A man beckoned from shore. He was dressed in the clothes of a voyageur, from the red toque on his head, to the moosehide moccasins on his feet.

"Bonjour!" The canoeman spoke! We paddled closer and learned that this was the headquarters of Voyageurs National Park. Hal Murphy was a guide for the North canoes.

"Ah, an express canoe! You must have a message from Montreal," he quipped.

"Not this trip," I responded. "We are on a journey of exploration."

Hal held out a hand and helped us ashore.

"We're taking a North canoe for a paddle in a while, would you like to sign on?" he asked.

We quickly accepted his offer. After spending much of the past weeks by ourselves, we were eager to paddle a large canoe with others. The North canoes floating in the water beside us were twenty-six feet long and almost six feet wide at the centre thwart. We chatted about the canoes until several other people joined us for the scheduled outing.

"Any non-swimmers?" Hal asked as we all climbed into a North canoe. Two people raised their hands.

"Good, you make the best voyageurs," he told them. "I know you'll stay with the canoe and keep paddling no matter what. Besides, you're replaceable . . . the cargo isn't!"

It wasn't long before we discovered that the craft was built for freight not comfort. The narrow seats were hard, with two paddlers sharing each board. During the fur trade, cargo would have taken up the little leg-room that was available. Each paddler had to sit tight against the gunwale to reach the water with their paddle. I wondered if the voyageurs ever traded sides, or if they just developed lopsided muscles.

Hal coached the novice paddlers and set the rhythm by counting out loud. Paddles clashed against others whenever someone missed a beat. Blades splashed in the water as the paddlers increased the tempo. Slowly, the canoe gained momentum.

The North canoe was not as easily turned with the stroke of a paddle as ours was. Hal stood in the stern and steered with a paddle much taller than he was. By shouting over the sounds of his wheezing crew, he communicated with his partner who stood in the bow with an equally long paddle. Working furiously, they each did several draw strokes on opposite sides of the canoe to change our course. The rest of us continued paddling.

Several hundred erratic paddle-strokes later, the crew accepted Hal's offer to rest in the shelter of tall marsh grass. While his eight paddlers caught their breath, he told tales of the voyageurs, dwelling on the hardships they had endured. I smiled knowingly when he talked of the long portages and the heavy loads. I rubbed my shoulders when he told of their eighteen-hour days. And I shuddered when he talked of hernias and drownings that took the life of many men. Then, as if on cue, a gust of wind shook the grass around us. It was time to head back. Paddling more smoothly now, we crossed the bay and glided to the beach.

"Next time, we'll challenge you to a race," Sally said to the others as we climbed back into our canoe. Paddling away at a fast clip, we appreciated the speed of our smaller craft. But as the first waves splashed over the bow, we had to admit that a North canoe would have been safer on the open water.

Our paddling tempo increased as we drew closer and closer to a reconstructed fort at the town of Fort Frances. Like voyageurs of long ago, we looked forward to a rendezvous and the celebrations that lay in store for us. This would be a chance to take a break from paddling, to feast and drink, to sing and dance.

After almost a month of paddling, we also looked forward to picking up a new pack of provisions. Our supplies had dwindled to little more than a chunk of pemmican and a small bag of flour.

The log palisades of a fort came into view as we rounded a point of land on Rainy Lake. Following a ritual of the voyageurs, I steered the canoe ashore so we could prepare for the rendezvous. First priority was a swim in the lake, where we scrubbed away the grime of countless portages from our bodies and our clothes.

We created a colourful scene. Each bush was adorned with clothes drying in the breeze: my maroon shirt on one, Sally's blue shirt on the next. Legs of our breech-front trousers dangled from branches, and our vests lay on sun-warmed boulders. Bright red sashes fluttered in the breeze.

While everything dried, we preened ourselves for the big event. First we cut each other's hair—quite a challenge with a small pair of old-style scissors. Then I trimmed my beard, peering into the shiny brass surface of a tinder-box. All went well until I attempted to shave my neck with a straight-razor.

"Zut alors!" I gasped. After a couple of nicks and yelps, I realized why many paddlers had rarely shaved. Cold water and lye soap made a poor shaving cream. Three nicks later, I decided my shave was good enough.

From packs under the canoe seats, we pulled out our second set of clothes saved for special occasions, along with colourful scarves and knee sashes. I took my red ostrich feather from between two pieces of bark and tucked it into my hat.

"How do I look?" I asked, strutting about.

"Like an ostrich in voyageur's clothes," Sally replied. I decided she was jealous of my top hat and feather. Her straw hat had lost its shape many rapids and rainstorms ago.

Late that afternoon, Sally and I canoed across the bay to the fort. As we neared the log palisade, I unfurled our flag at the stern of the canoe. It was important to look our best as we approached the fort so we increased the pace of our paddling and sang a lively French-Canadian song. The canoe surged ahead.

Had our approach been two centuries earlier, gun salutes would have rung from the stockade. Voyageurs and clerks would have gathered on the shore to cheer us on as we dug our paddles deep and pulled hard to impress the crowd.

No muskets flashed and no cannons were fired for our arrival, although a small but enthusiastic group on shore greeted us. That evening, in keeping with tradition, we were treated to a meal by the factor of the fort.

"The real celebration starts tomorrow," Pam Hawley said after supper. She was the curator of the fort and museum, and had arranged a rendezvous in our honour for August third.

Years ago, the North West Company fort had been the location of the yearly rendezvous for Northmen arriving from the Athabasca district. Voyageurs from this northern region had been unable to travel to Grand Portage and back before freeze-up, so this was their turn-around point. During the time it took clerks to sort and repack piles of trade goods and furs, the Northmen rested and partied. In fact, Alexander Henry had written: "The Northmen are treated as kings, during their time at the fort, and are regaled with bread, pork, butter, liquor, and tobacco, and such."

A rendezvous had the atmosphere of a carnival. Many voyageurs played cards or wagered on coloured rocks tossed into the air. Guessing games with an object hidden in the toe of a moccasin separated many a paddler from his hard-earned wages. Flute and fiddle music was accompanied by a rhythm section of revellers drumming on pots and pans.

There were usually few women at the rendezvous, but that didn't deter the men from dancing jigs and reels. The party would have grown wilder as the level of rum in the kegs became lower. The men had partied with abandon, making up for their dreary lives at remote posts.

To the Rendezvous!

Our celebration was as busy as any from the past. Through the day, visitors crowded around our tent and canoe. We sat on rum kegs and told tales of our journey, entertaining visitors with stories of wild rapids we had run.

Children ran through the fort, playing games of tag until lunch. Making *galette* was the highlight of their day as they rolled lumps of dough into long rope-like pieces between their not-entirely-clean hands. The children wrapped their dough around sticks and held them over a campfire until the dough was golden brown . . . or, in most cases, charcoal black.

Sally and I joined others in dipping our mugs into the pots of corn soup or raspberry tea. When Hal, our guide from Voyageurs National Park, arrived, I sized him up, thinking of challenging him to a wrestling match. He was only five foot four—I was several inches taller. Although he was well muscled from a summer of taking people on tours in the North canoe, he was also much older than me.

"I have paddled from Grand Portage. There is no stronger voyageur at the fort," I boasted, thinking I had a good chance of winning any test of strength.

"Ah, but my paddle propels a much larger boat," he replied, rising to the challenge. I'm sure I saw him wink at Sally when he suggested a shoving contest.

We strutted to the grass outside the fort. Before long, a crowd of onlookers materialized. Many of them knew Hal and were clearly on his side. I was the newcomer, the young upstart. Other than Sally, I had few people cheering me on.

Hal and I faced each other, each with feet braced in a wide stance and one arm outstretched. I locked fingers with my opponent.

"Push . . . push!" the audience urged as we each tried to force the other off balance. To my chagrin, there was no clear winner after three matches.

"Let's make it a bit more challenging!" Hal suggested.

This time we each stood on one leg, pulling and pushing. When Sally and the others collapsed in laughter at the sight of us hopping in circles, we decided to try a more manly contest—leg wrestling.

Ian and Hal wrestling

Party time at the rendezvous

To the Rendezvous!

We lay on our backs, hips touching, head-to-foot.

On the count of three I whipped a leg into the air and hooked ankles with Hal. Pulling sideways with all my strength, I tried to turn Hal onto his side. Then with one quick twist of his hip, Hal flipped me over.

"Not bad for an old voyageur," I conceded from where I lay sprawled on the ground. Two defeats later, I realized I should have chosen my opponent more carefully.

"Next we try the tomahawk throw. You can be the catcher!" he announced, laughing.

Later, we sat around a campfire and Hal recited a quote to the children, using a lilting French accent for emphasis.

"I have been twenty-four years a canoeman; no portage was ever too long for me. I could carry, paddle, walk, and sing with any man I ever saw. Fifty songs could I sing. I have saved the life of ten voyageurs, had twelve wives and six running dogs. I spent all my money in pleasure. Were I young again, I should spend my life the same way over. There is no life so happy as a voyageur's life!"

Hal's audience sat spellbound. It was easy to see how someone like Hal had been able to entice Quebec farm-hands into signing on as paddlers. I did notice, however, that the hardships that Hal had talked of when we were in the North canoe were not mentioned now.

After a while, Hal produced a flute and I joined him for a duet with my tin whistle. Several people danced around us as the sun set behind the fort. Later, someone brought out a bottle of wine and we each raised a glass to the paddlers of the past.

As the night sky darkened, the celebrations of our small gathering slowly came to an end. Fire embers faded. Yawns interrupted tales of wild rapids. Sally and I made our way to our tent and slept as soundly as any paddler had after a night of revelry.

Long after sunrise the next morning, Sally and I resumed our journey down Rainy River. We were a bit sluggish from too late a night and it took a while to get back into the rhythm of forty strokes a minute. It had been a grand celebration!

We were rudely brought back to reality when our paddling was interrupted only two miles downriver, at Chaudière Falls.

"I'd forgotten about this during the rendezvous," Sally groaned as we carried bulging packs of new supplies over the portage.

"That was probably the reason why Northmen were treated to such a great party . . . to be sure they'd sign up for another three-year term," I said, laughing. For the Northmen, winter, and second thoughts, would come much later.

We completed the portage, then drifted with the current, happy to be on our way again. It felt odd though, after a month of wilderness travel, to pass a settlement every few days where we could restock our food supply. Years ago, voyageurs had bartered goods or tokens for wild rice and corn. Sally and I eagerly traded coins for chocolate bars and ice cream—much-needed nutrients after weeks of limited rations.

Many travellers from the past had written that this was the most beautiful country they had seen. To homesick paddlers from Quebec, the flat, lush terrain reminded them of the farmland they had left behind. Low, verdant shores now replaced the stark granite of the Canadian Shield. Bald eagles swooped over the river as we paddled under canopies of maple, oak, and ash. It was a pleasant change from the predominantly coniferous trees we had seen so far.

The smooth eighty-mile flow of Rainy River was broken by only two rapids. The first was Manitou Rapids, where the river narrowed and became punctuated by a series of large waves. Even though an abrupt turn at a wall of granite added to the challenge of the rapids, we easily ran them in our loaded canoe. However, we thought it best to enquire about the Long Sault Rapids, a mile-long section of rough water just downriver.

We asked a local fisherman about rocks and other possible hazards at the rapids. He studied our birchbark canoe, then rubbed the stubble on his chin.

"I wouldn't worry about rocks," he said. "But I've heard stories of sturgeon ramming holes in small boats!"

We were sure he was exaggerating until the first monster fish leaped in an arc just ahead of the canoe.

"That one almost landed in the canoe!" Sally called as it splashed into the water.

Every time one of the large fish leaped out of the water, we thought of the fisherman's story. Fortunately, we missed every rock and every sturgeon in Long Sault Rapids and continued, unscathed, down the river, past the sites of Ash House, Hungry Hall, and other forts that had once dotted the waterway.

By August 8, a following wind nudged us on to Lake of the Woods. We eagerly dug out our sail, anticipating a free ride up the lake.

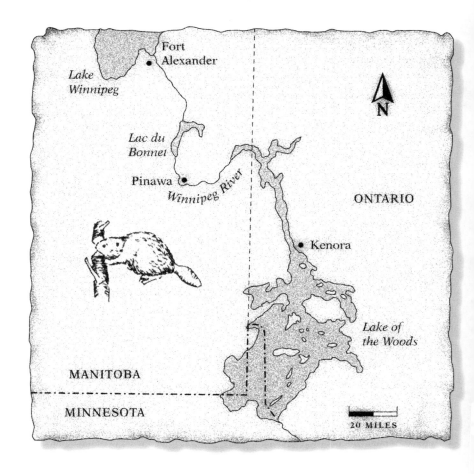

Fort
Alexander

Lake
Winnipeg

N

Lac du
Bonnet

Pinawa

Winnipeg River

ONTARIO

Kenora

Lake of
the Woods

MANITOBA

MINNESOTA

20 MILES

EIGHT

The North-West Wind

Souffle, souffle, la vieille!" I shouted skyward, echoing the words of voyageurs before us: Blow, blow, old woman of the wind. As wind-driven waves pushed our canoe from behind, I completed the ritual by sprinkling water from my paddle. Voyageurs might also have scattered an offering of tobacco on the lake for an extra measure of good luck, but we had to make do with a few crumbs of *galette*.

Voyageurs often carried a long pole as a mast for their sail when winds were favourable. We improvised by tying our tarp to two paddles, which Sally placed on each side of her seat. When the bottom edge of the tarp was anchored under her feet, she raised the makeshift sail.

"Hang on, we're in for a ride!" Sally shouted as she leaned back against the pull of the wind-filled tarp. The canoe surged forward at a speed we hadn't experienced since running rapids.

Every now and then Sally pulled the sail aside to peek ahead and make sure we weren't about to crash into something. She turned sometimes and looked my way for a moment, grinning from ear to ear. The crickets that had taken shelter in the upturned canoe during the night chirped louder and louder with each gust of wind.

As the wind propelled us up the lake, I thought that this was about as good as a voyageur could feel. Sailing was a time for singing and storytelling. Perhaps they just watched the gulls, as we did, soaring overhead while the canoes sped across the water.

"If this was a north wind we wouldn't be travelling at all," Sally shouted over her shoulder. Although I was less superstitious than the paddlers before us, I secretly hoped that sprinkling water from my paddle would ensure that the wind continued from the south.

Even with the wind directly behind us, sailing was not as easy as we had imagined it would be. Sally pulled against the sail with all her strength to hold it upright in the wind. I strained against my paddle, using it as a rudder to keep the canoe from being swept broadside by the following waves. And with the sail blocking our view, it was difficult to see where we were going. However, we were making terrific progress!

On calm days, the voyageurs often risked crossing the open water, heading directly for the north end of Lake of the Woods. However, it was not a decision lightly made, for it was a treacherous crossing. Many times, wind and waves came up without warning and caught paddlers on the open water.

Sally and I had chosen the somewhat safer, but much longer route among the islands along the eastern shoreline. To our left, the sandy beaches of Sable Islands stretched for several miles. To our right there was nothing but bulrushes and grasses—no solid shore or shelter, just a mat of tangled roots.

As the intensity of the wind increased, I watched each roller climb higher on the canoe until they reached the stitching at the gunwales.

"We can't stop," I shouted, the wind snatching the words away as I spoke. "If we don't . . . the same speed as . . . they'll wash over . . . "

Because the large sail obstructed Sally's view, she hadn't

realized how large the waves had grown. Now, she looked back. The expression on her face showed surprise, then dismay. We were surfing on a three-foot wave.

As the next wave caught us from astern, it lifted the entire canoe and carried us forward while the canoe rode on the crest of the wave. Moments later, the bow dropped into the trough between waves. The hull beneath my feet twisted and flexed. I thought back to when we had lashed the gunwales with spruce root; the care we had taken with each lashing paid off now. The canoe was tight and strong.

The next wave lifted the canoe and we surged ahead. Then came another wave, and another. It was a bit frightening to be propelled forward with such force, but thrilling at the same time. With hundreds of miles ahead of us, it was hard to resist progress that came so easily. By the time we stopped for the evening, we had covered forty miles with hardly a paddle stroke.

"More than double our usual distance!" I reported when I marked our location on the map.

"Here's to *la vieille* . . . and to another day of sailing," Sally said, raising her tin cup.

Despite our hopes, by morning the wind had switched to the north-west, chasing clouds across a darkening sky. We dodged from island to island, staying in sheltered water. Between islands, we encountered rolling, ocean-like swells. Coming broadside to the canoe, they were more sinister than the breaking waves that had accompanied us the day before.

Then a squall of cold rain blew across the lake. Like buckshot from a black-powder rifle, the raindrops spattered on the water. Voyageurs would have whipped off their shirts and tucked them under a canvas tarp to keep them dry. Many rainstorms ago I had discovered why: wet cotton sticks to skin, binding across the shoulders and making it difficult to paddle. Despite that, I chose to leave my shirt on. It was better to be hampered by wet clothing than to be stung by the driving rain.

Every few minutes, I paused to sop up the rainwater at

A full sail and following wind

Sailing on Lake of the Woods

my feet with a sponge. Then I gritted my teeth and resumed paddling.

"How's your straw hat doing?" I called the next time I stopped to sponge out the water.

"Wet," Sally replied in a monosyllabic grunt, her shoulders hunched and her paddle churning.

"Just trying to make conversation," I called cheerily.

"Great."

Even my spirits became dampened when I noticed water soaking through my felt hat. Luckily, the rainstorm stopped a short time afterwards. Our clothing and packs soon dried in the stiff breeze.

Four days of paddling later, we came to Turtle Portage, where voyageurs had carried their canoes and packs across an isthmus of land. As we tramped over the first portage we had encountered in more than a week, I realized this was another reason why many voyageurs had risked crossing the lake. With more than a ton of cargo in each North canoe, it must have been tempting to paddle across the open water, even in precarious conditions.

By the time Sally and I had progressed halfway up the lake, we were back into the land of white pine and granite shores. Cliffs rose directly from the water's edge for long stretches. In other places the rock had been fractured by winter ice and summer waves, leaving a shoreline of jagged, sharp-angled blocks.

Scores of treed islands added to the stark beauty of Lake of the Woods but made navigation a challenge. In fact, voyageurs had become lost more often on this lake than anywhere else.

"A few lob sticks to guide us would come in handy right now," Sally said as we paddled through one particularly confusing maze of islands and channels.

She paused from paddling to check the map again. "I'm not quite sure where we are . . . "

"Great! Imagine having to tell that to a crew of unruly voyageurs," I retorted.

"You *are* an unruly voyageur," Sally said. "Just keep

paddling north!" My comment must have touched a nerve. From that point on Sally checked the map frequently, noting our position each time we passed an island.

Even with the challenge of route finding, we enjoyed this part of our journey. Loons floated in many protected bays, their calls echoing against the granite shores. To the west, island after island punctuated the scene, their reflections shimmering like mirages on the water.

By mid-August, we reached the north end of Lake of the Woods. There, a short carry overland at Rat Portage north of Kenora brought us to the Winnipeg River. This had once been a river of spectacular rapids and falls coursing between walls of tortured rock. During voyageur times, twenty-six carrying places had marked its course.

Now, the character of the Winnipeg River has been altered by six dams. Sally and I didn't mind that there were fewer portages to interrupt our paddling, but we felt some regret that we would never be able to experience the whitewater that had challenged the voyageurs. With the higher river level, only a slow-moving current flowed in many places where rapids used to roar.

Although the river had changed, features along the way gave us a sense of what the voyageurs had seen. From the names they had given to land features, we recognized yellow rock and white clay along the shoreline. A dark hollow in a cliff still remained at a place the voyageurs had named La Cave. And farther downstream, at La Barrière, a rock jutted out into the river and created a narrow channel where paddlers had been forced to portage their gear.

With some trepidation we approached a set of rapids where Alexander Henry had lost a canoe, its entire cargo, and crew—in that order of importance according to his journal.

"That wasn't more than a whoop and a holler," Sally said afterwards. There was no longer anything but rolling waves where once rapids had roared.

"Wait till Eight Foot Falls. That should be a challenge," I replied. Yet even that wild-sounding stretch of water was just two whoops and three hollers worth of turbulence. And only a short section of whitewater rocked the canoe where Grande Rapide had been.

The lack of excitement on the river was more than made up for with sightings of wildlife. And our bark canoe, silently slipping through the water, was the ideal place to watch from. In one sheltered cove, we saw a doe and fawn browsing on willows. They peered back at us, curious yet wary. Farther downriver, we watched a fox trotting along the shoreline, oblivious to our presence.

Many times, we drifted past black bears perched in oak trees where they were dining on acorns. Beavers often accompanied us, occasionally slapping their tails on the water to warn others of our presence.

Late one evening, we decided to camp at a sandy bay where a solitary set of deer tracks led along the beach. Oak trees ringed the bay, but we noticed only a few broken branches and no recent signs of bears. The only danger appeared to be from falling acorns that squirrels were busily tossing to the ground. We reasoned that the squirrels wouldn't be so active if bears were around.

Sally and I ate supper with the trees at our backs, serenaded by the chirring of squirrels. Later, as we sat outside the tent drinking our last mug of tea, we heard the rattling of acorns showering down.

"Hope those squirrels don't keep us awake all night," Sally said.

I was nodding my agreement when we were suddenly startled by the sound of breaking branches from the trees behind us. Nervously, we looked over our shoulders. Only a few strides away, an enormous black form was climbing down an oak tree.

"Bear!" Sally hissed under her breath.

We froze. Would the bear retreat or attack? How fast could we launch the canoe? Luckily, the bear seemed as frightened as we were. We remained motionless as the bear scrambled down the tree and loped into the bushes. When the crashing of branches diminished, I let out my breath.

"Let's get out of here!"

Sally leaped up and began tossing gear out the tent door. "No sense waiting to see if the bear comes back for a midnight snack," she said. Working quickly, we jammed our belongings into canvas bags and collapsed the tent.

Canoeing to another campsite was out of the question. We'd had difficulty finding this spot and knew there were few potential campsites on the rocky shore. Daylight was dwindling, and we didn't relish the thought of being caught on the river in the dark.

Hoisting our packs, we walked along the shore, not sure which way the bear had gone. Ten minutes later, after stumbling over fallen trees and through tangled bushes, we paused to light our candle-lantern.

"This light will keep the bear away," I said bravely. By the weak glow of the flickering candle, we continued our search for a place to pitch the tent.

The moonless night had become darker than the inside of a tinder-box when we came to a small clearing where beavers had felled some trees.

"There's just enough room between the trees for the tent," I announced after taking two long paces to measure the clearing.

"Looks good—as long as the beavers don't drop a tree on us," Sally countered, pointing to a partly chewed aspen.

After considering our options, we decided to risk the possible dangers of beaver-felled trees. To discourage our web-footed neighbours, we wrapped canvas tarps around the trees nearest the tent.

Sally and I slept lightly, waking now and then to noises in the forest.

"What's that?" Sally said as she clutched my arm. I tensed and listened for a bear, hardly daring to breathe. Then I heard it. Something the size of a mouse scurried through the dry leaves near our heads.

Later, we were wakened by the sound of beavers slapping their tails on the water, just off shore. We decided that their tail slapping must have been in response to the sight of our

Early morning on the Winnipeg River

A voyageur camp

tent, because no beavers ventured onto shore near our camp.

We paddled away the next morning unscathed by bear or beaver. However, those worries paled in comparison when, two campsites later, we were visited by a creature that would have struck fear into any voyageur. A creature so sinister that the strongest, bravest paddler would have tiptoed away, quaking in his moccasins.

After hearing a strange noise outside the tent, I cautiously open the door and peered out. In wide-eyed horror, I watched a skunk amble past, sniffing like a dog following a scent. Its white-striped tail, held high, passed the door only inches from my nose. I held my breath.

"What?" Sally said loudly, awakened by the sniffing. The skunk whirled around in fright, then, thankfully, scooted off without spraying us. I let out my breath and then shared my tale of terror with her.

On this sparsely settled stretch of the river, we saw four-legged creatures more frequently than people. The few people we did meet greeted us warmly and usually offered treats after hearing our descriptions of dried food and corn mush. A woman at the Point du Bois portage contributed cinnamon rolls hot from the oven. We had hardly licked the icing off our fingers when an elderly Cree woman at Grand Falls presented us with a bag filled with freshly baked oatmeal cookies.

"A person can take this pemmican thing too far," Sally said the next afternoon, happily munching a chocolate bar that a couple passing by in a boat had given us.

Fuelled by these extra treats, we reached Pinawa a few days later. Here, voyageurs had two routes to choose from, depending on the water level. They could paddle and portage along the Winnipeg River, but this was often a treacherous route strewn with wild rapids. Or they could take the safer, but more arduous Pinawa River and rejoin the Winnipeg River at Lac du Bonnet.

Alexander Henry's account of the Pinawa River did little to inspire us to take this shortcut: "The stream of the

Pinawa is shallow, with scarcely sufficient water for the Craft to swim. Its bed is rocky and broken; the carrying places are eight in number, through mud and marsh. The mosquitoes were here in such clouds as to prevent us from seeing our course at times."

The voyageurs had sometimes camped near Pinawa while their guide scouted the route ahead. Sally and I camped here as well, and were transported back in time when twenty members of the Manitoba Living History Society held a feast to celebrate our arrival. One man was clothed from head to toe in buckskin, and a Métis woman wore a traditional black and red wool dress. Others were dressed in the colourful outfits of voyageurs or early settlers.

Someone produced a shovel and dug a pit for a fire, cloths were spread out on rough-hewn tables, and stumps were rolled into place for chairs. Shortly after, the cooking crew arrived bearing spits, skewers, enormous fry pans, and a cauldron.

Sally and I edged closer to the fire, inhaling the smells from the sizzling fry pans. By the time supper was cooked, my stomach was growling almost as loudly as the bear that had visited us a few nights earlier. Eagerly, we lined up for our ration of roast, corn soup, fried onions, and potatoes.

"A toast to times gone by," a top-hatted gentleman called as we sat down to dinner. Pewter goblets of high wine were raised and a cheer went up from the group.

High wine had been a much-traded item during the fur trade. Its main ingredient was rum diluted with water and coloured with tobacco or iodine. I remembered reading that pepper, tincture of opium, and even sulphuric acid had sometimes been added to the alcohol.

The home-made high wine served at our feast appeared to be of a much higher quality, although it had a strange, metallic taste.

"Are you sure there are no unusual ingredients in this wine?" I asked our host, after dutifully testing two mugs of the brew.

She laughed. "It's your tin mug reacting with the acid," she explained.

The feast continued until late evening. By the time I had polished off the last piece of blueberry pie, I was drowsy and sated, glad that our tent was only a few steps away.

After another day of rest, Sally and I were eager to continue our journey. We rose at the first flush of daylight the next morning. Although it was only early September, the night had been cold and a thick fog swirled along the river, rising from the water that was warmer than the air.

After packing up camp, we pushed off into the void. The only sounds that broke the silence were the rhythmic splash of our paddles and the low burble of the bow wave. Our senses came alive as we drifted down the river, watching for the dark forms of rocks.

We seemed to float in a space between water and sky, a barely discernible line between the two elements. Alone on the river, there was no sense of time, of place. It was easy to imagine that we were paddling two centuries earlier— the canoe, the water, and the rhythmic splash of paddles would have been the same. White fog banks swirled, then lifted as the sun warmed the air. The black silhouette of a shaded shoreline stood in stark contrast to the bright, sunlit fog.

As the fog cleared, mergansers and mallards flushed up from quiet backwaters along the river, wings whistling as they flew low over the water. Drifting with the current, we gazed at high river banks of swaying grasses and shrubs, topped with stands of poplar. Beyond, but out of sight, were farms and small settlements. From canoe level we felt only the solitude of river travel.

The current of the river came to a standstill at Lac du Bonnet, then gradually picked up again as the lake narrowed. Days slipped by as we continued past St. Georges and Pine Falls, and finally, three portages later, Fort Alexander. This had been the site of a North West Company pemmican post where voyageurs had stopped for provisions before the long journey on Lake Winnipeg. Sally and I picked up supplies here as well, and packed another three weeks of food in our canoe.

Each time we had stopped on the Winnipeg River, people had warned us of the dangers ahead on Lake Winnipeg: the shallow boulder-strewn shoreline, the wicked winds, and the canoe-capsizing waves. The warnings had become more and more dire as we moved north.

Just as we were leaving Fort Alexander, one grizzled boater sized up our birchbark canoe and felt compelled to add his piece.

"You're asking for trouble in a small boat like yours. That lake is a mean one. If she doesn't bring a fist of a wave down and capsize you, she'll split your boat in two when you hit bottom," he said in gruff, ominous tones.

Sally and I looked at each other. Capsizing waves? Canoe-splitting lake bottom?

"That was as good a tall tale as any voyageur's," I said, shaking my head and chuckling when he had left. With his words of encouragement ringing in our ears, we paddled towards the big lake.

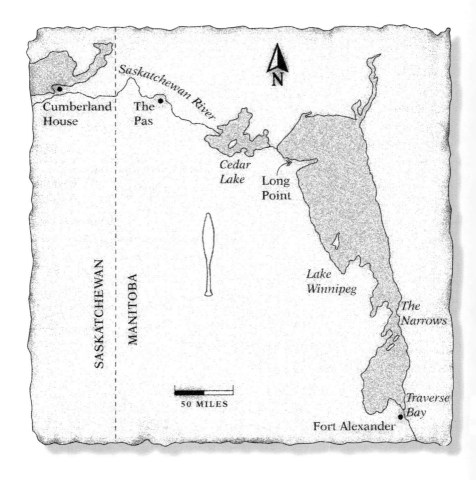

Cumberland
House

The
Pas

Saskatchewan River

*Cedar
Lake*

Long
Point

*Lake
Winnipeg*

*The
Narrows*

SASKATCHEWAN

MANITOBA

*Traverse
Bay*

Fort Alexander

N

50 MILES

NINE

Lake Winnipeg

Viewed from canoe level, Lake Winnipeg is overwhelming in its scope. As we looked north, water and sky merged at a thin, barely discernible line on the distant horizon. Between our canoe and the horizon was only a huge expanse of cold, grey water. There was not a boat or a bird to be seen.

"It looks more like the ocean than a lake," I said in awe. From our map, we knew the lake was almost three hundred miles long and up to sixty-five miles wide. However, the map had not prepared us for the scene before us.

Feeling very small, we began paddling around Traverse Bay at the south end of the lake. Although the name implied that voyageurs had crossed the bay, we were reluctant to venture far from shore. Even so, we were forced farther and farther out as the lake became too shallow to paddle.

As we canoed a mile off shore, I became aware of a dark band of water moving towards us. Just as I began to ask Sally if she had noticed the unusual pattern on the lake, a blast of wind snatched my words away. With frightening speed, the calm water we had been paddling across grew to whitecaps.

Waves sloshed over the gunwales as we struggled to turn the canoe around. Then, like a leaf on the water, we were driven back down the lake by the wind—to the exact place we had started an hour earlier.

"Do you think that man back at Fort Alexander was right?" Sally asked as we unloaded the canoe in the surf.

"Well, I'm not laughing any more," I replied, looking at the unsuitable campsite where the waves had forced us ashore. The thick bush bordering the lake was impenetrable, so we hauled our gear as high as possible up the beach.

The canvas tent billowed like a sail in the wind as we struggled to set it up. While Sally held the tent from becoming airborne, I anchored it with long sticks driven into the soft sand. We stacked a wind-break of driftwood beside the tent then waited for the storm to pass.

Voyageurs had called this period of sitting out a storm a *dégradé*. It was a degrading experience because wind and waves had got the better of them and their plans. Secretly, they probably enjoyed a respite from days of paddling that began before dawn and frequently ended long after sunset.

As daylight dwindled, Sally and I lay in the tent listening to the howl of the wind and the roar of rollers crashing on the beach. More disconcerting were the sounds of canvas flapping and poles creaking as the tent walls were sucked in, then puffed out again with each blast of wind.

Suddenly, a stentorian gust tore a front peg from the sand.

"It's on your side," Sally mumbled, pulling the blanket over her head.

As the loose corner flapped wildly, I scrambled outside. Luckily, we had piled some sticks by the tent for a fire in the morning. This time I drove two long sticks through each loop of the tent.

For the remainder of the night I slept fitfully . . . dressed and ready to leap to action if the tent pegs were torn loose again. As the wind gusted higher and higher, I had visions that we would be blown—tent, blankets, clothing, and flailing bodies—across the open plains.

At daybreak the wind still howled and the canvas tent

shook like a wet dog. When I peered out the tent door I saw, to my horror, that the lake had risen to within two paces of our camp. Waves lapped at one end of the canoe, despite the fact that we had carried it high up the beach the night before. We hadn't been warned that strong winds could drive the water from the north end of the lake, raising the level at the south end.

The strong winds forced us to spend another day on shore. In an attempt to calm *la vieille*, the old lady of the wind, voyageurs might have cast trinkets into the lake. But I learned that she wasn't easily calmed when her mood was blustery. If anything, the wind increased after I made an offering of an antler button.

To pass the time, Sally and I paced the narrow beach, tossed rocks at driftwood targets, and wrote in our journals. Mostly, we caught up on our sleep. We were exhausted from the past weeks of paddling.

The storm ended by morning and we continued on our way, more wary of the powerful lake than before. When we came to an exposed headland, dark rocks jutted out from the water like the hulls of shipwrecked boats. Gulls wheeled overhead, mewing eerily.

"Let's keep going," I urged when Sally's pace began to slow. This was not a place I cared to linger as we paddled our small, vulnerable craft.

Luckily, the calm weather held, and by the following day the lakeshore was more hospitable. White, sandy beaches stretched as far as we could see. Thousands of terns and gulls flushed up from sandbars when we canoed past. They lifted in one mass and circled over us, calling and swooping and gliding on the currents of air.

As we canoed along the west shore, Sally and I settled into the steady paddling rhythm necessary to travel long distances. Our blades entered the water together and swept back in unison. Sally paused while I did a J-stroke to keep the canoe tracking straight. Then our red blades arced forward with a spray of drops and re-entered the water.

Every few minutes, one of us called out "change." After

the next paddle stroke, we switched sides without missing a beat. The paddling we had done so far this summer had built the muscles necessary to maintain this pace all day.

"If only we had other voyageurs to race against," I said as the shoreline slid by all too slowly. Sally and I talked about the race of races that had taken place between North West Company canoes on this lake. Taunts had been hurled back and forth for days. Reputations were at stake. During the race, there had been no time to rest, no time for songs. Guides, caught up in the excitement, had hacked off hunks of pemmican, which the straining voyageurs chewed as they paddled faster and faster. Paddles flashed at fifty, then sixty strokes a minute. In that race, the competitors had canoed for an astounding thirty-six hours without stopping until they were ordered to rest.

"Singing would be a less tiring way to break the monotony," Sally suggested. To pass the time, Sally and I sang until we were hoarse.

En roulant ma boule roulant, en roulant ma boule.
C'est pour en faire un lit de camp, en roulant ma boule.
Rouli-roulant, ma boule roulant, en roulant ma boule . . .

Paddling northward, we also sang to mask the apprehension we felt on the open water. Our first hour on the lake had taught us that the wind could come up without warning. In the back of our minds was the fear that we would be unable to land our canoe safely if wind and waves caught us off a boulder-strewn shore. This tension, plus the tedium of paddling mile after mile along a shoreline with little variety, began to wear on us.

"Stop rocking the canoe!" Sally complained as we paddled against the wind for the fourth day in a row.

"Okay, if you put more pep into your paddling," I shot back.

There comes a point on any long journey when weariness sets in. We had been paddling forty strokes a minute—more than two thousand per hour. If the wind remained moderate we would pull on our paddles more than twenty thousand times by the end of the day. And yet, with all that

Seagulls on Lake Winnipeg

The vast expanse of Lake Winnipeg

effort we were not getting any nearer to a visible goal. From canoe level, the lake appeared as immense as ever.

I wondered aloud about how the voyageurs had felt with blistered hands, sore backs, and wet feet. The joys of the last rendezvous would have been long forgotten. Except when storm-bound, the paddlers would have no days of rest until they reached their destination. Did tempers flare? Did fights break out? Did they become weary, as we did, of always travelling, of sleeping on rocks or sand or pebble beaches?

"The last thing I want to think about right now is voyageurs," Sally snapped. I stopped mid-sentence, annoyed with her response. After all, it was their life we were reliving.

Neither Sally nor I spoke for the next hour until I declared it was time for a shore break and abruptly turned the canoe. Without a word, we anchored the canoe, then walked to opposite ends of the short beach. We sat with chins in our hands, brooding silently. After many long minutes, I looked over to Sally. She smiled weakly and thumbed her nose at me.

"I guess it's a bad idea to argue with the only other person in a hundred miles," I conceded when I walked over to her. She put her arms around me, squeezing tight.

For the next four days, the lake remained comparatively calm, with only two afternoon winds that blew us off the water. We paddled hard, putting miles and miles behind us. Finally, we were making some progress.

Just north of The Narrows, the respite ended. Wind howled along the low shoreline, broken by only a few scraggy trees. Waves tossed higher and higher. As the roar of wind and waves reached a crescendo, Sally and I pulled hard against our paddles.

Heads down and backs bent to the task, we struggled towards shore. Waves washed over Sally as the canoe rose up, then smacked down into the trough between each swell. As the canoe dived into the next trough, I thought of the warning we had received about being dashed to pieces when the canoe hit bottom.

"We have to abandon ship!" I called. No sooner were my words out than my end of the canoe hit bottom with a thud.

Shouting into the wind, Sally suggested that we should both jump out at the same time to avoid swamping.

"After this wave . . . " she called, the wind snatching the words away as she spoke. I tensed my legs.

"Now!" We leaped into waist-deep water just as the wave swept past. The next wave almost knocked Sally over. When it passed, the water dropped to our knees. We struggled to maintain our balance and hold onto the heaving gunwale of the canoe.

Finally, we made it to shore. Still fighting the waves, we unloaded the canoe in the churning water. As Sally tried to steady the bucking canoe, the gunwale banged against her legs again and again. She didn't dare let go.

Working as quickly as possible while struggling to maintain my balance on the slippery, uneven rocks, I ferried each pack to shore. I was near shore with the last pack when my left foot slid between two rocks. As I stumbled forward, a throb of pain came from my ankle. Without thinking, I uttered a French curse, then limped back to retrieve the canoe.

"Ready . . . hup!" and the canoe was on our shoulders. We stumbled to shore and placed it under a wind-blown tree.

Sally and I collapsed under the twisted pine and compared battle scars. Already, Sally's battered legs were turning purple. My ankle was red and swollen.

"I seem to recall that injured voyageurs were left behind at native camps to recover. If they survived the winter, they were picked up the following spring on the return trip," Sally said as I soaked my ankle in a pot of cold water.

"You wouldn't leave me behind, would you?" I asked.

"Only if your arms give out," she replied. I smiled wearily at that vote of undying love.

"My arms are fine, but at the rate we're paddling, our food will give out before we reach the north end of the lake," I said.

This was as good a time as any to bring up the topic. After

two weeks on Lake Winnipeg, we had been wind-bound almost as many days as we had paddled. We were less than halfway up the lake, and had only seven days of food remaining.

Alexander Henry had experienced similar problems on Lake Winnipeg. Even with a large crew of paddlers in a North canoe, it took three weeks to travel up the lake. His journal of 1808 tells the tale:

August 10th Suddenly the wind opened up a gale. Before we could land, our Canoes were half full of water, and all of us wet to the skin. One of my canoes, from hitting bottom, was split asunder from one Gunnell to the other.

August 12th At two o'clock a squall appeared from the S.W. We had great difficulty in reaching Land. The rain fell in torrents and the wind blew a hurricane . . .

August 13th During a long traverse, the wind rose suddenly from the west, and the swell increased . . . Our position was decidedly unpleasant. The sea dashed with great violence against the rocks and we shipped a great quantity of water before making shore.

August 14th Blusterous weather. Dégradé.

August 15th . . . A sudden squall from the N.W. obliged us to put ashore at L'Isle d'Encampement . . . My tent was blown down and we passed a wretched night, wet to the skin.

August 16th . . . The swell was so high that, in rounding a point, we came near to capsizing. Our baggage was completely soaked, and thus we spent the evening by the fire drying our packs.

August 17th . . . After much trouble in loading, we embarked . . . Almost every swell ran over the canoe. Soon as we could find bottom all hands jumped overboard, each taking a load on shore.

The next two entries in Alexander Henry's diary told similar stories. Packs were opened and the contents spread out on the rocks to dry. Blankets and materials were draped on nearby trees and bushes. After eight days of wind and waves, the weather finally moderated. Wind-battered and hungry, the voyageurs had continued up the lake.

Sally and I sat in our tent, wondering if our experience might duplicate the voyageurs' eight-day layover. The gale was so strong we'd had trouble remaining upright on one of our brief forays up the beach. The entire lake was a churning mass of white-capped waves and the air was heavy with mist blowing off the lake. Although we remained in the tent for much of the day, we didn't feel rested, only tense from the constant fury around us.

On our second day my diary entry was short and to the point: "September 14th. Another wind day. Bored and frustrated." Nothing else needed to be written.

By our third morning of sitting out the storm the wind had diminished slightly. Impatient to make some progress, we packed up camp and began canoeing north. We paddled for less than an hour, far from shore to avoid rocks and shallow water, when a gale suddenly blasted from the north-west.

Adrenaline surged through my veins. Within minutes we were bucking the highest waves we'd encountered so far. The wind roared in my ears. Sally shouted something, but the wind whipped her words away.

A gust of wind grabbed the high bow and drove the canoe sideways. The next wave smashed into the canoe. The hull shuddered with the impact. As the canoe keeled over, we reached out and braced with our paddle blades flat on the water. Water surged over the gunwale. Just as I thought we were going to tip, the canoe stabilized.

We angled the canoe into the waves, fighting against them to reach shore. My arms ached and knees were bruised where they braced against the side of the canoe. Sally's waterlogged hands were numb.

As we neared land Sally and I searched for somewhere to get off the lake, but all we could see was an inhospitable rocky shore. The canoe dropped into the next trough and my paddle struck a rock, almost wrenching it from my grip. One wave later, Sally and I leaped into the icy water to prevent the canoe from hitting bottom.

Once again, we fought our way to shore, hauling the canoe behind us. Once again, we unloaded the canoe in the surf, standing almost waist-deep in cold water.

Wind-chilled and waterlogged, Sally and I carried the canoe to the beach. I knelt to start a fire with a pile of driftwood we had hurriedly collected. As the flames flickered in the wind, Sally and I crouched over the fire, sheltering it with our bodies.

"We almost didn't make it to shore that time," I said quietly.

"I know," Sally replied.

The rocks were cold, the water was cold, and the wind was cold. I jumped up to secure a flapping tarp in the wind and returned to find that even my tea, which I had so looked forward to, was cold.

My mood reflected our bleak surroundings. The scene consisted of two elements: churning water and featureless shore. Even the birds had flown elsewhere. Sensing my dark mood, Sally kept her distance—not easy on a beach only two canoe-lengths long.

That evening we spread the map across the tent floor to see what lay ahead. The chart was water-stained and worn from two weeks on the lake. I looked over to Sally. Her clothes looked almost as water-worn and tattered as the map.

We huddled in the confines of our canvas shelter as tempestuous gusts of wind shook the walls. When the fury of the gale increased, we discussed the risks of paddling the rest of the lake.

Two exposed points farther north had been named Point Maligne and Point Formidable with good reason. There were few bays or protected areas on the long, low shoreline. On this part of the lake, the voyageurs had made a total of ten open-water traverses, each five miles or longer, between islands or points of land.

The greatest hazard lay at the north end of the lake where Long Point jutted twenty-five miles out from shore. The voyageurs had called this Le Détour, and rounding it was often dangerous. Over the years, several fur brigades had been caught in squalls gusting down the lake. Many canoes were driven onto the rocky shore and dashed to pieces.

"I vote we make our own detour . . . and live to paddle another day," Sally said quietly.

Remembering all the journal accounts of this lake devouring large North canoes, I agreed it was not prudent to continue in our small craft. With the sound of surf roaring in our ears, we decided to bypass the treacherous north-west shore of the lake. Our next challenge would be to paddle against the current of the mighty Saskatchewan River.

TEN

To Cumberland House

As we stood on the north-west shore of Lake Winnipeg, I wondered what voyageurs had felt when they realized it was now upriver to wherever they were headed. After surviving the winds and waves of Lake Winnipeg, it must have been discouraging to see the relentless current of the Saskatchewan River surging towards them.

"I bet the new voyageurs weren't told of this when they signed up," I said to Sally.

"Ha! Neither was I," she replied.

Just upriver from where we stood, wild torrents of water had once tumbled over a limestone escarpment. Two hundred years ago, voyageurs had portaged around the Grande Rapide and the Roche Rouge Cascade. Now a dam stands where waterfalls had blocked the voyageurs' way.

Above the dam, Cedar Lake floods the valley, forming a hundred-mile-long maze of channels and islands where rapids used to flow. Stumps and deadheads bob in the water, like ghost canoes of bygone days. Piles of jumbled driftwood resemble voyageurs resting on shore. Thick clumps of bulrushes line the shoreline, like rows of paddles stuck in the mud. It is an eerie and desolate scene, with none of the grandeur of long ago.

Near The Pas, the Saskatchewan River narrows. From Alexander Henry's journal, we learned that this part of the river is the same now as then—swift, silt-laden water, muddy shores, and willow-topped banks. From this point, only eighty miles of upriver travel lay ahead of us. However, the current that we paddled against was becoming stronger each day.

Our progress dropped to sandpiper speed. In fact, we could barely keep up with these diminutive shorebirds as they walked along the beach. At one stretch of fast water, the sandpipers ran ahead, leaving us to struggle against the current.

"At least we're going faster than the mussels," Sally reassured me.

Although the only visible sign of each mussel's movement was a weaving line left in the soft mud, I wouldn't have bet my day's ration of chocolate that Sally was right. A brief pause to catch our breath and we lost all forward momentum; another moment to remove a layer of clothes, and the river carried us backwards.

"Back-eddy!" Sally announced when she saw slower water on an inside curve of the river. It was worth our effort to cross to the other side, where the reverse current would carry us upriver and double our speed.

The shores were so muddy that we paddled for several hours before finding a place to stop and stretch our legs. Time after time, we nosed the canoe into the river bank and Sally leaned out to test the firmness of the shore with her paddle.

"Not here," she said at a likely looking spot, when her paddle sank to the top of the blade. The sand that had looked so inviting concealed bottomless mud.

As the days passed, Sally and I learned to study the animal tracks to gauge if the shore was soft or firm. Otter slides indicated soft, slippery mud. Deer prints dotted the river bank where the shore was firmer, although moose seemed to wander to the river anywhere, punching deep holes in the mud. The depth of beaver tracks and the troughs left by the branches they had dragged were the best indicator of the softness of the shore.

We climbed out of the canoe one evening at a river bank where wolf tracks barely left an imprint. Because Sally was lighter, she offered to carry the bags from the canoe—a good plan until she picked up the first heavy bag. Before she could take a step, the mud was halfway up her boots.

"Ian, help!" she called. Seeing her predicament, I ran along the shore to collect driftwood for a mat to stand on.

"Hurry, I'm still sinking . . . "

I would be no help to Sally if I also became mired in the mud, so I carefully laid a path of branches to the canoe. By the time I reached Sally, she had sunk almost to the top of her boots.

"Now, what was that comment you made about leaving me behind if my arms failed?" I teased as she reached for my hand.

"Just pull me out!" she grumbled.

Sally leaned on me while I grabbed her left leg and heaved upwards. Her boot popped out with a loud slurp and a spray of muddy water. With one foot on the platform of driftwood, she was able to pull her other foot free.

We decided to continue up the river and try our luck elsewhere. That evening we had to settle for a sandbank bordered by a dense jungle of willow. At least there was no mud. I pushed the tent stakes into the soft sand and hoped for a windless night.

Alexander Henry had experienced much the same conditions when he travelled this way with a North West Company brigade. He wrote: "It was so unpleasant as to have mud up to the middle whence we unloaded. The last rain form'd the mud into a kind of mortar that adheres to the foot like tar, so that at every step we raise several pounds of mud. Every thing that touches it, receives its share, so that in a short time my tent and its contents were compleatly daub'd."

"Some things haven't changed a bit," Sally said when I

read the passage. Through the summer as I had read the words of Henry's journal, we'd come to feel a bond with this person we knew only through printed words. From wild rapids to sticky mud, not only had we followed in his footsteps, but we had also experienced similar trials and triumphs. It no longer seemed just a coincidence that we were experiencing the same things. It was as if we were travelling together. In a way, Alexander Henry had become our mentor. Sally and I could almost feel his presence as we looked out over the muddy banks of the river.

Fortunately, our journey upriver had more to offer than merely mud and muck. The autumn colours of late September were at their peak, adding bright splashes to the scene. Leaves of crimson and gold swirled in whirlpools and floated in quiet eddies. Yellow groves of poplar lined the high banks, and flaming-red bushes bordered the river. Forests of dark spruce stood in stark contrast to the colours around them.

With the cooler weather, we began to see migratory birds heading south. Flock after flock of snow geese flew over the valley, white V's etched against the blue sky. Gaggles of Canada geese circled as they descended to land at the marshes beside the river.

In the tent that evening, we listened to the sounds around us: the whistling wings of teals flying low over the water and the rusty-hinge croak of cranes high overhead. Every now and then, we heard the two-syllable call of Canada geese as they headed south.

"Think they know something we don't?" Sally asked, nestling up to me under two layers of blankets. Light from a harvest moon filtered through the trees, casting a shadowed pattern of spruce branches on the walls of our tent. Each night was becoming colder and we were glad to be getting close to Cumberland House.

Sally was up first as usual the next morning, even though a layer of frost edged the blankets.

"Hey, the moccasins are frozen," she said, trying to pull a stiff lump of leather onto her foot. A few minutes later she returned and announced that thick ice had formed on the pots of water.

When Sally crawled back under the warmth of the blankets, I took that as a hint that it was my turn to light the fire. The night before I had stacked kindling and birchbark under the canoe to keep dry. Now I laid them in a depression scraped in the coals of our previous fire. From my fire-lighting pouch, I removed a curved piece of steel and a chunk of flint. Then I opened a brass tinder-box and took out a small square of charred cloth. Although we had matches in our supplies, I enjoyed the ritual of lighting a fire with flint and steel.

In my left hand, I held a corner of the charred cloth over the flint. As I struck the steel against the flint a spark flew up, then faded away. I tried again. This time a spark landed on the cloth. Gently, I blew on the spark until a button-sized glow of red appeared.

I laid the piece of cloth on a nest of shredded birchbark, then coaxed the glow to a flame. As the flames grew, I added more bark, then kindling. I leaned back, closed my eyes, and savoured the aroma of wood smoke.

Somehow, the routine of lighting a fire took me back in time more than any other aspect of our journey. The flint, steel, and charred cloth were a link to the days when survival in the North Country depended on knowing how to coax a tiny spark into a flame.

Sally and I sat close to the fire, dressed in every layer of clothing we had with us, including wool mitts Sally had sewn from a blanket months earlier. We reminisced about our journey and how much we had learned about the voyageurs by living as they had.

"You know, there's only one thing I can't figure out," Sally said, reaching out to warm her hands over the fire.

"What's that?" I asked, expecting some great revelation as we neared the end of our canoe journey.

"Why didn't the voyageurs have pockets in any of their clothes?" With that deep thought, she leaped up to pack up camp.

We hadn't paddled far before our passage was blocked by two sets of rapids. At the first set we were able to make some progress by sneaking from boulder to boulder in the calmer water near shore. We pulled hard on our paddles, perspiring with the effort of paddling against the current. In the eddy of the first boulder, we removed our toques. Next stop we took off our sashes and blanket coats.

"At this rate, we'll be naked by the time we reach the top of the rapids!" I remarked when we removed our vests.

At the second set of rapids we struggled up the river for many minutes, trying not to look at the tree that remained beside the canoe no matter how hard we paddled. We fully agreed with the voyageurs' principle of avoiding a portage whenever possible, but this was becoming a losing battle with the current. We drifted backwards then pulled ashore.

Voyageurs had used several means of advancing upriver when the current became too strong for paddling.

"How about poling up the river?" I suggested, remembering that it had been the voyageurs' favoured method.

"You mean standing in a tippy canoe . . . in the middle of the rapids . . . while pushing poles into the soft mud?" Sally asked.

It didn't sound like such a great idea worded that way. We had tried it once in slower water and found it required perfect balance and coordination between the person at the bow and the person at the stern.

Another method was lining a canoe. With long hemp ropes attached to the bow and stern, voyageurs walked along the shoreline, pulling the loaded canoe upriver. The only consolation was that it was rarely muddy on the rocky shoreline where rapids occurred.

The theory of lining is simple: trudge along the shore with the canoe in tow, keeping the bow pointing away from shore at a slight angle to the current. In reality, it is not as easy as it sounds.

"I'll walk ahead with the longest rope," Sally volunteered, after we had tied ropes to the bow and stern.

Lining up the Saskatchewan River

Rapids near Cumberland House

126

After a few minutes of upriver travel, we realized our ropes weren't long enough. Several times, we had to wade in the river to keep the canoe from grinding over boulders near shore. We danced from one slippery rock to another as we hauled the canoe upriver.

Progress was slow but steady until we reached the next curve in the river. As Sally let out her rope, the bow of the canoe swung out from shore.

"Pull the canoe in!" I shouted over the roar of the rapids. When Sally turned around, she saw the canoe was almost broadside to the current and about to be sucked under.

The pressure of the water made it almost impossible for her to hold the bow rope. I released the last inches of my rope just as the water reached the top of the gunwale. With one tremendous heave, Sally pulled her rope in to point the canoe upriver again.

During the seconds it took Sally to regain control of the canoe, I had visualized our bags and packs bobbing down the river all the way back to The Pas. I laughed out loud when I thought of all the wild rapids we had negotiated on our long journey. It would have been a sorry end to the trip to have our canoe capsize, going upriver, only a short distance from our destination.

"Let's take a break," I said when our heartbeats returned to normal. During our shore break, I noticed smoke in the distance. I looked more closely and saw houses partly hidden by bushes.

"Hey, that must be Cumberland House!" I announced.

"I knew we must be getting close, but somehow I'm not ready for this to be our last day of canoeing," Sally said, following my gaze upriver. As we talked, we realized that we each felt an odd mix of emotions—elation at being so near our goal, and sadness that our canoe journey was almost over. We decided to camp where we were and enjoy one more night on the river.

After supper that evening, we sat by the blazing campfire under a canopy of poplar and aspen. Firelight reflected on the yellow leaves, and we lay back, listening to the occasional swirl of the river as the powerful current coursed past.

Later, we pulled out our maps and completed a ritual that had been part of our life for nearly three months. With a fingertip, I traced the blue line of the Saskatchewan River as it meandered back and forth across the pages. I wrote *October 5* on the map and drew an arrow to our position on the river. Seeing how far we had travelled was a rewarding way to end the day.

Like Sally and me, some of the voyageurs would have ended their canoe journey at Cumberland House. I wondered if they had looked forward to winter as much as we did, with thoughts of dog teams racing across untracked snow.

For those men stopping at Cumberland House, their arrival was a time of celebration, of toasting each other, their guides, and even their canoes. For many voyageurs, native wives and families eagerly awaited their return. After an absence of five months or more, it would have been a joyful homecoming.

Other voyageurs would have pressed on, even though it must have been tempting to stop and join the festivities. As nights became colder and days shorter, those paddlers became even more eager to get to their own posts before winter. Many were still a long way from their destination— perhaps Île-à-la-Crosse on the Churchill River, or distant Fort Chipewyan on Lake Athabasca. Their biggest fear was an early freeze-up of northern lakes and rivers that would prevent them from reaching their goal.

Sally and I woke at dawn to the soft patter of wet snow on the canvas roof of the tent. I peered out the door and saw the curve of the river, barely discernible in the snowstorm. In the snow-blurred distance, the canoe-like form of a snag bobbed in the water. Years ago this would have been another canoe racing us to the trading post.

To Sally's surprise, I was up first. On this last morning of our canoe journey, I did something I had wanted to do all summer. I collapsed the tent while she was still in bed.

"Levez, levez!" I called. "Winter waits for no paddler!"

Building our birchbark canoe

Canoeing on Rainy Lake

Hauling our canoe upriver

Portaging the canoe

Lunch on the water *Re-gumming the canoe*

Canoeing on Lake of the Woods

A voyageur meal of galette and pea soup

Dancing at the rendezvous

End of the day

Favourable winds

Sailing on Lake of the Woods

133

Running flat out

Showing Sting the map

Tea break along the way

Travelling on the Saskatchewan River

135

Ian and Buck

Ready to go!

A cozy camp at minus 30

ELEVEN

Life in a Northern Post

As Sally and I paddled towards Cumberland House, the howling of sled dogs echoed across the river. To us, that sound was as grand a welcome to the north as any travellers had ever heard.

Inspired by the howling, we increased our paddling tempo for the last hundred strokes to our destination. We cached our canoe and gear on shore, then changed out of our mud-caked clothes and set off to explore the village.

Cumberland House had the slow-moving character of many northern communities. Children and dogs roamed up and down the dirt road, and a few mud-caked pickup trucks rattled by, every driver waving at us as they passed.

"Looks like our kind of place," Sally said, pointing out that almost every house had a canoe, dogsled, or snowmobile in the yard.

In the centre of the village stood a brown, fort-like building. This was the North West Company store, complete with the historic crest above the door, the same crest that we had painted on our canoe. On a bench outside the door sat an old man wearing a faded wool shirt and work pants. His gnarled hands told of a life outdoors, and hand-beaded moccasins told of his heritage. When he nodded a greeting, Sally and I went over to say hello.

"Getting too cold for canoeing, isn't it?" he asked. News travelled fast. We had talked to only one person on our walk to town.

"Cold weather is just what we're looking for," I replied. Then I told him of our plans to continue by dog team and toboggan during winter, to follow the trails that voyageurs had taken.

He leaned on his cane, and a faraway look came to his eyes. "I used to travel that way," he said. "When the snow comes, I'll tell you some stories."

Moïse told us this was the old-timers' bench, and we could find him here most days with his friends. Sally and I assured him we would be back to hear his stories, then wandered inside the store.

The North West Company store revealed much about life in this remote community. In addition to aisles with food and clothing, we saw bolts of cloth, boxes of beads, and piles of cookware that had been a northern post's stock-in-trade for centuries. Along the back wall, we saw axes, ammunition, dog harnesses, parkas, and winter boots.

As in the past, the store also served as a bank and a trading post. Several people were lined up at the back counter, paying their accounts or asking about their balance on the ledger.

"Wha' canna do for ye?" a man asked, with a broad Scottish accent as we walked up to the counter.

I couldn't help nudging Sally with my elbow ... a Scotsman? Like days of old? We were dressed the part of paddlers, so I did my best imitation of French-Canadian patois as I told him of our long canoe journey from Grand Portage.

The man's expression was one of amused astonishment. When I drew breath, Sally interrupted, giving her account of our trip and purpose, without the accent.

Arnold Shields leaned against a desk and crossed his arms as we told our tale.

"Did you know I was recruited as a clerk when I was a lad not yet twenty?" he began. "The company came to Scotland, as they had every year for centuries. And so I signed on in the spring of 1967."

Sally joined in. "I knew the North West Company was founded by a group of Scottish traders, and that recruiters used to go to Scotland. But I didn't think that still continued."

"Aye," said Arnold. "Right up till when I joined . . . and then some." Arnold explained that the rugged life in Scotland produced young men who were well suited for outpost life in Canada. The new recruits were frugal, hard-working, and accustomed to a simple diet.

"We were used to hardships," he said. "Many houses in Scotland weren't heated, and my father insisted the windows stay open for our health even in the coldest weather." For many recruits, including Arnold, the woodburning stoves in the remote posts would be an improvement over the peat fires back home.

When Arnold was recruited, the company was hiring single men seventeen to twenty-three years old. His parents had to attend the meeting, and the first question the recruiter asked was if they would agree to let their son go to Canada.

"During the interview I was asked how many brothers I had," Arnold said, thinking back many years. A third son was a desirable candidate because he had few obligations at home and would not be in line to inherit the family business. If a young man was engaged or had a steady girlfriend he was turned down because of the risk that he would become homesick and desert his post.

To our surprise, Arnold still had his original contract, the one he'd signed more than thirty years earlier in Scotland. The contract was similar to the ones we had seen from two hundred years ago. There was still a blank space to insert the number of years a recruit agreed to serve, and another space for the yearly wage. I smiled when I read the words stating the recruit had to agree to do nothing that would bring dishonour to the company. And, like contracts of long ago, Arnold's parents had to sign beneath his signature.

"Being a true Scotsman, I came for the money," Arnold added, pointing to the yearly stipend inked on the contract. "They offered double what I could earn back home . . . and a chance to become a factor in charge of a trading post after a two-year apprenticeship."

Arnold and the eight other recruits from his area had no real sense of where they were going or what to expect, he told us, but I guessed that many had been drawn by the adventure. And quite an adventure it was—three days after arriving in Canada, Arnold was clerking in a remote northern community.

"I had second thoughts when I arrived at the post at Island Lake," he admitted. "It was May, and there was still deep snow on the ground." Island Lake in northern Manitoba was a small settlement, linked to the outside world by bush-plane or boat. In the winter, freight came in by tractor-train over the frozen muskeg.

Sally and I were surprised to learn that Arnold's daily chores included hauling water, chopping wood, and keeping the stove going through the day. Nevertheless, the simple life appealed to him and he readily adapted to his first winter in Canada.

"Weren't you homesick after a while?" Sally asked.

"Aye, I was at that," he replied.

"Well, what kept you here?"

Arnold rubbed his chin thoughtfully. "Oh, the company promised all the recruits that they would get back the travel costs they had deducted from our wages, with interest, if we stayed for two years. I was determined to get that money," he explained.

Arnold brought a photo from a shelf near the till. "But she's the real reason I stayed. I still remember the day this young Cree woman walked into the trading post. Her name was Rita and I was smitten." He smiled, recalling the past.

Sally smiled, too. "I read that years ago, the North West

Company had encouraged recruits to marry local women so they would stay . . . "

Arnold interrupted, chuckling. "Well now, there's nothing in the handbook about that. Although marrying Rita certainly kept me from going back to the old country!"

We stood to one side for a few minutes while Arnold served a man wearing hip-waders and smelling of fish. He accompanied him to a rack of fishing supplies and helped him choose several lures. Arnold handed another customer a file for sharpening an axe, then returned to continue his story.

When we asked Arnold about the present-day store, we learned he still buys and sells furs as part of his business. Many of the North West Company stores also buy crafts and carvings, as well as hand-made moccasins. These days, the stores pay cash instead of the tokens or the barter system of the past, although a good deal of the money is returned to the store through purchases. Until a few years ago, trappers could still get an advance and be outfitted with ammunition and supplies.

By the time Arnold had told his story, it was late afternoon and the store was becoming busy. Sally and I stocked up on fresh produce and chocolate bars, then headed back to the canoe.

Mixed rain and snow was falling when Sally and I pitched our tent at the river. With little discussion, we quickly decided our next project would be to find permanent shelter for the winter. I briefly thought of asking Arnold if he needed an apprentice, hoping that housing might come with employment. But an indoor job was not for us.

"If only we could be hired on to deliver the mail by dog team from post to post," I said wistfully.

"Nice thought, but not in this century. Besides, I read that the dog drivers had to sleep with the dog teams— outside the fort!" Sally replied.

The next morning we started our search for a place to stay. I began by scanning the two-page phone book for some ideas. The names revealed the mixed heritage in the community starting with the French-Canadian influence: from Carrière, Chaboyer, and Deschambeault, to Goulet and Laliberté. At the *M*'s, the Scottish influence became apparent with several listings of McAuley, McGillivary, McKay, and McKenzie. We learned later that of twelve hundred people in Cumberland House, almost half were Métis—a mix of Cree, French, and Scottish ancestors.

While I phoned hunting and fishing camps, hoping someone might have a cabin to rent, Sally chatted with every person who wandered into the North West Company store. I was contemplating starting at the *A*'s and working my way through the phone book when Sally tugged at my sleeve. She announced that someone had suggested there might be a room available in the old convent.

"Putting up trail-weary voyageurs in a convent . . . sounds so French-Canadian!" Sally said, delighted.

Sure enough, we were able to rent a small room there until February, when we would embark on the next leg of our journey. A truck dropped off our boxes of winter equipment two days later. Although I had assured the caretaker we were just quiet writer-types, I had downplayed the volume of winter camping equipment that we expected. She seemed a bit dismayed when Sally and I hauled box after box of gear up the narrow staircase. In no time our room was crammed with canvas bags, boxes, and piles of winter clothing.

"Wait till she sees the twenty bags of dog food coming next month," I whispered to Sally. Then I tiptoed down the stairs for the last load.

It felt good to stay in one place for a while, within walls that didn't flap in the wind, and under a roof more substantial than canvas. And yet, in the back of our minds we knew that by midwinter, wanderlust would strike again and we would be eager to travel. Meanwhile, we were happy to unpack our bags and to organize our belongings into cupboards, knowing we wouldn't have to repack the following morning.

A dusting of snow a few days later reminded us that we should prepare the canoe for the winter. Alexander Henry had mentioned that by early November, his canoes were "already much split by the severe frost." Sally and I were horrified at the thought of our canoe being split in two after all it had survived on the way to Cumberland House.

Among the books that we had packed were several old journals, which we consulted to find out how voyageurs avoided this problem. Some told of burying their canoes in the ground to protect them from the elements. We preferred the method that most voyageurs had adopted: knocking the ribs loose to take the pressure off the bark and then stowing the canoe under cover.

We asked around until we found somebody with space in a shed to store our canoe. Once in the shed, we gently tapped each of the ribs loose, working from the centre to the ends of the canoe. Until spring thaw, the canoe would hang from the rafters, safe from severe weather and animals.

I reached up and ran my hand over the bark.

"Remember this?" I asked Sally, pointing to a scuffed area at the widest part of the canoe.

"Thanks for reminding me!" she laughed. "That was our first set of rapids—before I learned how wide the canoe was." It seemed like a lifetime ago, hundreds of thousands of paddle strokes earlier in our journey. We reminisced about our summer experiences, then walked back to town with renewed enthusiasm for the challenges that lay ahead.

Over the next days, we continued exploring Cumberland House. At the north end of town, in a small clearing among spruce trees, we found a stone-walled building originally used to store gunpowder. It was the only remaining building from an old trading post.

Samuel Hearne of the Hudson's Bay Company had been the first to build a fort at Cumberland House in 1774. Until then, the company had relied on trappers bringing furs to faraway posts on Hudson Bay. Britain had granted the company a charter in 1670 for exclusive rights to trade in the Hudson Bay watershed. However, independent traders had been intercepting many of the trappers, forcing the Hudson's Bay Company to build their first inland post.

Joseph Frobisher of the North West Company quickly countered with a fort only a stone's throw away from Hearne's post at Cumberland House. This was an ideal location for another fort in the Nor'Westers' extensive network of inland trading posts. With water routes extending from this point north to the Churchill and Athabasca regions, west to the Rocky Mountains, and east towards Montreal, Cumberland House became an important resupply depot.

I tried to visualize what the clearing would have held back then. Each fort had been surrounded by a log palisade with a sturdy gate. Alexander Henry's journal described several buildings inside the fort, including a trading house, storehouse, workshop, and a number of other log structures. The rough-hewn buildings had featured sod roofs, windows of animal hides, and curtains of burlap.

His words brought the scene to life: "Men having finished cutting our stock of fire wood, now making dog sleighs for later use. Desmarais employed bending snow shoes . . . Other men employed sawing boards and squaring timber, Smith making nails, some making soap, others sturgeon netts. Soon I shall send the men out to raise dog trains."

The clearing was quiet now. The only sound was the crunch of frozen moss under our feet; the only sign of life was a field mouse that scurried under the stone foundation.

Sally and I continued our walk to the current North West Company store to see who might be sitting outside. Several grey-haired men usually "warmed the bench" as they said, watching the world go by. Moïse Dussion, Charlie Fosseneuve, and Solomon Goulet were always good for a yarn or two about the old days.

After our first visits, Sally and I had learned to slow down, to match the pace of northern life. We learned not to interject comments or questions in the long pauses between sentences. Many times, the pauses merely meant they were translating their thoughts from Cree to English.

We asked about the trading post of years ago. It was Moïse's turn to weave a tale.

"Back in the 1940s, the post had lots of trouble with free traders who came to our camps to buy our furs and sell us groceries and other things. It was good for us, because we didn't have to travel all the way to the post. But then, The Bay bumped the price from fifty cents to five dollars a muskrat, to drive away the competition. The free traders couldn't match that!"

Moïse paused to catch his breath and Charlie took over. "When the free traders left, the price suddenly went down to fifty cents again. We didn't sell our furs, but kept them, hoping the price would go back up."

Moïse continued. "My uncle was hired by The Bay to take a letter by dog-team express to the post at Pine Bluff telling them that the muskrat price was now back down to fifty cents. He went with two friends and stopped around the corner from Pine Bluff." He paused and smiled, the corners of his eyes crinkling as he thought back to those days.

"Well, the other two guys went to the post with three bundles of muskrats and sold them all. Maybe two or three hundred muskrats at five dollars each. They made lots of money!" He burst into laughter, accompanied by the other men on the bench.

"When they came back around the corner, my uncle went to the Pine Bluff post with the letter saying the price had dropped to fifty cents. The manager was mad when he found out, but he couldn't do anything."

I could tell that the men on the bench had all heard the story many times before, but a new audience made it worth telling again. They enjoyed talking about old times, and felt that life had been simpler in the days when they could hunt and fish for most of their food.

"We caught whitefish in the fall, then we would hang them to dry. That was our winter food. We would get ducks too, when they were fat. The women would salt them and hang them to dry. Now people buy their meat in cans," Moïse said with a shake of his head.

They also talked of the days before the gravel road that links Cumberland House to other communities.

"Back in the sixties Cumberland was all boats and horses and dogs and mud," Charlie said. "In the winter, people would come from Barrier or Pine Bluff by dog team just for a dance. Dances would last until two or three in the morning, sometimes to sunrise. We danced reels and jigs to fiddle music."

"Say, are you going to the feast tomorrow?" Charlie asked. When I said we hadn't been invited yet, he shrugged and said, "Neither has anybody else. They put up a note at the post office and people just show up."

With that informal invitation, Sally and I went to the feast. We added our contribution to the table then looked over the other items. The table sagged with bannock and beans, dishes of wild rice, and other country foods including sturgeon, grouse, goose, and duck.

I looked at a plate of dark meat, wondering what it might be.

"What's this?" I asked the man beside me.

"Moose meat," he replied quickly.

"And what part of the moose is this?" Sally asked, selecting a finger-long drumstick from the same plate.

"Hind quarter," he retorted. Everyone burst into laughter.

The feast was a wonderful opportunity to meet the people of Cumberland House. When word got around that we planned to stay for the winter, several people offered us country food and invited us to drop by and visit.

As the days passed, daylight hours dwindled and many people spent their evenings playing bingo or cards. A game of cribbage with Arnold and Rita was always good for a laugh or two. Listening to his brogue as he counted made me think of Scottish clerks years ago, sitting around a table, playing cards by candlelight.

By the end of October, our life in Cumberland House settled into a quiet routine. Between visits with new friends, Sally and I read books about the fur trade and the voyageurs. Often the accounts would prompt me to write a page or two, or inspire Sally to sketch in her journal. Many days included a stroll to chat with the old-timers sitting on the bench.

When the weather became colder and a thin layer of snow blanketed the land, the men frequented the bench less often. Winter would soon be here. It was time for Sally and me to start "raising a dog train" as voyageurs had long ago.

TWELVE

Colder Days

"Snowshoe weather coming," Charlie said from his bench, eyeing the white flakes floating down from a grey sky. "Mushers used to make their own snowshoes, you know."

He looked me square in the eye, as if issuing a challenge. Then he smiled mischievously. Sally and I didn't even have dogs yet for our planned winter journey, but it seemed, at that moment, that snowshoes were a first step to becoming mushers.

"Do you remember how they were made?" I asked.

Charlie nodded his head slowly, and leaned forward. That was our cue to settle on the bench for a long story. He described how small birch trees had been split in half and carved for frames, and how moosehide had been scraped then cut into strips to lace the snowshoes.

"Any ideas where we could get a moosehide?" Sally asked after Charlie had finished his story. Charlie mentioned that he had seen someone smoking moose meat, and we might find a hide there.

Charlie's hunch was right, and it turned out that the man who had the moosehide was happy to give it to us. We lugged the hide home, then sought out elders who still remembered how to make babiche, the lacing for snowshoes. They explained that our first step should be to scrape the hide clean.

I fashioned a stretching frame of sturdy poles and tied the hide to it. Carefully, Sally scraped away at the hide with a hatchet. Word of our moosehide project spread through the settlement, and people began stopping by to watch us work.

"This is hard work but I'm getting there," Sally said as a new visitor approached the stretching frame.

"I know," replied the older woman with a smile. "I've been watching you from my window all morning."

Philomene didn't say much, but after some time she bent down and picked up the hatchet Sally had been using. Without a word, she started scraping, pulling down with the hatchet in rapid, short strokes.

"Not like this!" she said with a chuckle, pretending to strike the hide with a sharp blow of the hatchet.

"How much should I scrape off?" Sally asked.

"When you're down far enough you'll see lines, like veins," she said, running a hand over the leather.

A while later, one of the regulars from the store bench came by. Solomon sat on a stump talking with me as I carved a snowshoe frame with a crooked knife. Sally was working just two paces away.

"I used to make my dog harnesses from moosehide," he told us. "I made a tube with the leather and then stuffed in moose hair for padding."

"Really?" I said, interested. "We're thinking of making our own harnesses, too."

Solomon's eyes twinkled. "Before you start, maybe I should bring my dogs over and show you how much they like to chew on moosehide!"

"I don't want to slave over some harnesses just so the dogs can eat them," Sally protested. After Solomon continued with more stories based on the dog-eating-gear theme, we decided to buy harnesses made from less tasty material.

A few mornings later, Charlie dropped by to check on our progress. I looked up from my snowshoe frame and smiled as he talked to Sally; this was becoming quite a community project. After all, the sight of people working on a moosehide or making snowshoes was uncommon these days.

After Sally had scraped off all the hair, we let the hide dry. Then, using a sharp knife I cut a pencil-wide strip, going around and around the hide. A couple of hours later, almost two hundred feet of lacing curled about my feet.

The next step was to bend the wood I had carved. With the knowledge we had gained from bending canoe ribs, Sally and I tackled the snowshoe project with confidence. We heated a tub of water over a fire and boiled the pieces of wood so they would be pliable enough to bend.

Three hours later, Sally pulled a length of birch from the tub and handed the steaming wood to me. I began coaxing it around a bending jig we had made.

"More hot water!" I said urgently. Sally poured water over the wood, which was cooling quickly in the near-freezing temperature. The birch was not as flexible as the cedar for our canoe had been, and the extra pot of water we had on the fire didn't last long.

I strained to bend the wood into the correct shape. Suddenly, it broke with a loud snap that made us jump.

"It wasn't me!" Sally spoke up quickly. We laughed as we remembered her trick of breaking a stick as I bent a canoe rib.

"Guess that's why we made spares," I said sheepishly.

We boiled the remaining frames for another two hours and tried again. Now the sun had chased the chill from the morning air and this time we had a large pot of water ready by the fire.

With one smooth motion, I bent the toe around the jig while Sally poured a steady stream of hot water over the birch. Then I eased the birch around the gradual taper to the tail. As Sally clamped the wood in place, I heaved a sigh of relief. The next three frame pieces also bent easily,

Preparing moosehide for snowshoes

Lacing a snowshoe

perhaps because they had been heated for much longer than the first one.

After the frames had dried for a few days, we drilled holes at the tips and tails, then lashed the pieces together at both ends with babiche. Now came the part we had been most worried about—figuring out how to weave the complex criss-cross pattern of babiche in the snowshoe. Using a pair of borrowed snowshoes as a model, we started.

Over, under, over. Over, under, over. Loop, twist, change direction. Slowly, the snowshoe began to take shape. Hours passed and we became totally absorbed in the task, not even noticing that we'd skipped lunch. As we tied the final knot in the babiche, Sally seemed lost in thought.

"You know, I think it's the learning that I enjoy most about our trips," she said, after gazing at the snowshoe she held in her hands.

"Not the long portages or rain?" I teased. "Actually, you're right. I love learning about the old ways of doing things, learning of a way of life that is almost lost."

I thought back to all the adventures we'd been on . . . and realized that learning was the element that linked each of our journeys. As Sally and I worked on the next snowshoe, we savoured the process, every twist and loop of the babiche. We finished at midnight, tired but content, and one step closer to our winter trip.

Charlie and Solomon were the first to see our handiwork the next day. Charlie held a snowshoe up, studying the lacing pattern. When he nodded his head and smiled, we knew it had passed the test.

"You're almost ready for winter," he said. "Now all you need is a toboggan!" He glanced at Sally and I was sure I saw a conspiratorial wink. I had a feeling Sally would suggest we build a toboggan from scratch for our next project.

"My grandfather used birch to make toboggans, too," Solomon added, as he inspected the other snowshoe.

"Really?" Sally asked, her interest piqued.

"Green wood was best, but it had to dry for a month or two before you could use the toboggan."

"Two months? We'll need a toboggan before then," I countered.

"Well, the North West Company used to stock bent-boards so people could make their own toboggans, even in midwinter," Solomon added. That sounded like a project we could tackle. But where would we find bent-boards these days, I wondered.

After dozens of phone calls, we finally tracked down one of the few remaining toboggan-makers in Canada. A week later, crammed in with the weekly truckload of groceries for Cumberland House, our toboggan parts arrived. A bemused driver unloaded the cargo of pre-bent boards, a roll of sisal rope, a backboard, and an enormous canvas bag, called a *carriole*.

Sally and I pored over old drawings to get an idea of how the three-board toboggan was rigged. The toboggan-maker had included some instructions, but it still took us a full day to string the ropes, attach the canvas bag, and secure the backboard.

When it was finally assembled, we stood back to admire our winter transportation. It was twelve feet long by eighteen inches wide. The knee-high canvas bag stretched from the curl at the front to the backboard. In the confines of the shed, the toboggan looked much larger than we would need.

"You stand at the back, and I'll sit at the front," Sally suggested. "Then we'll get a better sense of the toboggan's size."

"It doesn't look too large, after all," I observed when we were in our places. The *carriole* bag was not much bigger than the cargo space in our canoe. By the time we packed bulky winter clothing and camping gear, I had an idea the bag would be full.

Later that day, I asked Solomon to check our toboggan and confirm that we had assembled it properly. He studied it from one side, then stood at the back and gripped the handles. The backboard needed to be more upright, he advised.

Finally, he tugged on the ropes.

"You'll break your toboggan," he stated matter-of-factly. We learned that the ropes needed to be loose enough to allow the toboggan to twist and flex over rough trails. He informed us that sisal rope tightens as it becomes wet. We would have to check the tension every few days.

Solomon picked up a length of rope and started to braid the fraying end while we looked on. His father had hated long, messy strands of unravelling rope and had taught Solomon this skill. Now, he passed the knowledge on to us. Solomon also showed us how to make a "snub rope" to anchor the toboggan to a tree with a quick-release knot.

"Practise this knot," he advised, reviewing the twists and turns. "Because if it doesn't release you'll have to cut the rope!" I made a mental note to keep a hunting knife handy in the toboggan bag.

Solomon stayed for a while, talking about dogs as Sally and I coated the boards with linseed oil so they wouldn't absorb water.

"We plan to run the dogs single file," I said, when Solomon asked how we intended to hitch the team to the toboggan.

"That's the best way for a freight team. I still like the look of dogs running in line," he answered, his eyes lighting up. "I had a well-dressed team with bells, pompoms, and streamers. The dogs could tell when they were dressed up. They were proud!"

As Solomon shared his memories with us, we learned that he had used a five-dog team to haul heavy tubs of fish. His toboggan had been identical to ours except for a moose antler he used for a brake. Our snow brake was a metal hook. Solomon helped us attach it to the toboggan with a braided length of rope.

With the toboggan now properly rigged, we began making cold-weather clothing from heavy blankets we had packed with our winter gear. For my winter coat, Sally used a four-point trade blanket, the largest that had been made. The pale-blue blanket featured a band of dark blue at each end. Four lines, called points, woven into one side indicated the blanket's size and value. Originally, each point had represented the trade value of one beaver pelt.

Voyageurs from different parts of Quebec often wore a colour representing their region. Sally grew up in Rigaud, Quebec, so she chose the red blanket, as voyageurs from that area had used long ago. The blue blanket for my coat was the colour Montrealers had worn. Those from Trois-Rivières had favoured the white blankets with multi-coloured stripes.

Following a pattern we had acquired from a museum, Sally and I laid out each blanket so the stripes would be around the bottom of the coats as well as the cuffs. After sewing hers together with a blanket stitch, Sally modelled the coat.

"Well, there's certainly lots of room for sweaters," Sally said, engulfed in the huge wool *capote*. The bottom edge hung below her knees and the front flaps overlapped by at least a foot. A wide, woven sash held the coat closed and took some weight off her shoulders.

We were pleased to learn from Solomon that an outfit like ours was very warm. To keep the wind from chilling us on blustery days, he suggested making canvas covers for our blanket coats. Solomon also told us that we could make thigh-to-ankle leggings that winter travellers had worn from the remnants of each blanket.

"How did you hold up the leggings?" Sally asked. In all our reading, we hadn't found a satisfactory answer to that question.

"Some people just used sashes around their knees, but I also tied the top of the leggings to my belt with a cord," Solomon said. That made sense to me. Solomon added that the leggings had been used only in the coldest weather for extra insulation.

On this visit, Solomon showed us the pompoms he had used on his dogs. Each fist-sized ball was made of tufts of different-coloured yarn and topped with streamers.

"Just like the voyageurs!" Sally exclaimed. When Sally and I had been doing our historical research, we had seen an old painting of colourfully clad voyageurs and their dog teams. In the painting a number of men were leaving a fort, running behind their dogs and loaded *carriole* toboggans. The dogs were gaily dressed in beaded blankets with pompoms and bells on their harnesses. The men wore long knitted toques and striped blanket coats with bright red sashes. From the first time we saw the painting, we had daydreamed of stepping into the scene and running with the voyageurs.

With that vision in our minds, we added pompoms to our list of projects. Following Solomon's instructions, we spent a few evenings rolling up old socks and attaching colourful tufts of wool to make our pompoms. Eight socks and several skeins of wool later, Sally surveyed the pile of multicoloured, striped balls.

"All we need now is a dog team," she announced.

"And some snow!" I added. That was almost as important an ingredient as dogs.

By late November, there was enough snow on the ground to inspire us to look for dogs in earnest. Sally and I visited several mushers, asking if they had extra dogs at a price our budget adventure could afford. We were looking for the type of dogs that voyageurs would have used—strong, freight-pulling dogs with thick fur. We also hoped they would be mild-mannered. Although we had travelled with a team of huskies years ago, Sally was uncomfortable with aggressive dogs.

We started with John Carrière. The Carrière family had been raising dogs for generations, and he took great interest in our upcoming journey.

"We're hoping to travel for six weeks by dog team, from post to post, as voyageurs had," I said when he asked about our plans. Our goal was to cover about six hundred miles, camping out each evening as we followed the old trails that linked the remote posts.

"Well then, you'll need at least five big dogs," he said. We learned that John's grandfather used to do the mail run by dog team, and as a boy, John had made many trips with him.

"I thought I'd just ride on the toboggan the whole way . . . but he brought me along to break trail for the dogs!" John added, chuckling as he remembered his days on the trail.

These days, John's dogs pull lightweight racing sleds. The huskies of long ago had been bred to leaner, faster dogs for racing.

"We're looking for males," I said when John pointed out several females he thought would be suitable. I agreed with the theory old-time trappers had expressed, that a female in heat could cause fights among the other dogs. I also reasoned that male dogs are usually larger. John wasn't convinced.

"If you put a female up front, all the other dogs will run faster!" was his reply. It was a good argument, but we decided to stick with our decision.

Of the dogs John was willing to part with, we liked a long-legged male, the only one that looked large enough and strong enough to haul a heavy toboggan.

"That's Jeff, he's a leader," John said. I looked at Sally. Her eyes told me that she liked this gentle, quiet dog. Jeff became the first dog in our soon-to-be team.

Our next stop was at Chip McKenzie's dog yard. Chip and his wife, Denise, both remembered their fathers running dogs on the trap line and knew the kind of dog we were looking for.

"This one is too young for heavy work," Chip said, passing by a likely looking canine candidate.

"Hank is a bit too slow for us, but he'd be good for you," he said when we approached a friendly looking dog. Sally reached out and he immediately grabbed her mitt and ran to the far side of his stake-out area.

"If we take him, do I get my mitt back?" Sally asked. Chip laughed, then named a fair price for the dog and mitt.

We appreciated Chip's candid honesty about his dogs. "Tom's only got one eye and he's a bit old—but he does have four legs!" We quickly agreed that having four legs was an important feature, and decided to take him.

Chip selected two more dogs, named Buck and Blue, who

were too slow for racing but suitable for our journey. Including Jeff, we now had five dogs for a team. Still not quite sure what we were getting into, I shook Chip's hand to close the deal. Then Sally and I headed into the forest to clear underbrush from the area where we would keep our new family.

The dogs were a bit apprehensive when we led them to their new home the next morning. They tugged at their leashes . . . not afraid, yet not quite sure what was in store for them. Once at our dog yard, we clipped the dogs to individual chains so they had plenty of room to run around.

Each dog pawed and sniffed at the fresh straw we had laid out. Then they explored every inch of their new territory, circling round and round, chewing at twigs we had left uncut, and, of course, peeing on the tree in the centre of their stake-out areas.

As each dog sniffed and marked his territory, Sally and I took stock of our new team. Jeff was tall and skinny, with hip-bones that stuck out from his frame. Buck was noticeably bow-legged and appeared to have fleas. Tom was old, blind in one eye, and his teeth were worn from years of chewing bones and frozen meat. Blue was young and, like a teenager, his legs seemed too long for his body. Hank the nipper looked as though he had been on the wrong end of a few nips himself, with a torn ear and scar across his nose.

"They're perfect!" Sally gushed, slipping her arm around my waist.

THIRTEEN

Dog Tales

At feeding time, five previously shy dogs lost all their inhibitions. When I approached with bowls of food, each dog began barking, yelping, and lunging against his chain.

"I think they like us!" I said to Sally, shouting over the din. In reality, I knew it was the food that excited them. By feeding the dogs and spending time with them, we hoped to gain their confidence. Our plan was to spend a week with the team before attempting to hook them to the toboggan.

This time would also give Sally a chance to become comfortable with each dog. She would need that time, I realized, when I saw her looking at Tom, but standing just beyond his reach.

"He sounds so aggressive," she declared, as he barked loudly at her. "I'm worried he'll bite."

"Tom's just glad to see you," I said. "Why don't you feed him for a few days and get to know him better?"

After the frenzy of feeding, Sally and I visited each dog. We started with Tom, who was calmer now that his stomach was full. He was actually quite an attractive-looking creature, with black fur tinged with brown on his nose, eyebrows, and feet. Tom was the smallest of our dogs, but his way of exposing his teeth when he barked flustered Sally.

Luckily, Sally was more comfortable with the other dogs—even Hank the nipper. In his excitement, Hank tugged at mitts or pants any time we ventured within his reach. He was a little taller than Tom, and his husky-like colouring was more brown than black.

We next visited Buck, who lowered himself in a fawning manner when we approached. Buck was another husky mix, with large feet, a cream-coloured face, and big brown eyes. When Sally reached out to pet him, he jumped up from a crouch and gave her a wet lick across her face.

"Yecch, dog breath!" Sally groaned, wiping her face on a sleeve.

In comparison, Jeff was a bit reserved, but seemed to be a gentle creature. He watched our every move intently, ears perked forward at the sound of our voices. Jeff was light-coloured, tall and lanky, with a trace of collie in his features.

Finally, there was Blue. He was the largest and youngest member of our team, all black except for white socks and pale blue eyes that seemed wolf-like when he stared at us. He was the most active, bounding and leaping high into the air when we approached.

Their characters became even more apparent when we tried to measure them for harnesses the next day. Jeff stood reasonably still, patiently tolerating the measuring tape that we passed around his chest and neck and along his back. However, the other dogs acted as though I had a whip in my hand rather than the harmless length of tape.

"How many inches?" I asked as I stretched the tape-measure along Blue's back.

"I'm not sure," Sally replied. "He moved when I was trying to read the number!" Four attempts later, we had the measurements we needed.

After Blue, we moved on to Buck. He squirmed, he jumped, and he wriggled as I tried to restrain him long enough to get his measurements. Just as Sally was reaching under his chest, he licked her face from chin to eyebrows.

"Not again . . . you'd think I would learn!" Sally groaned, toppling backwards. And so it went as each dog performed various contortions while we attempted to record accurate measurements. Luckily, Hank was last, because he chewed the measuring tape, obliterating the numbers from fourteen to twenty-four.

"I've got it!" Sally said triumphantly, writing down the last numbers. The moment the words were spoken, Hank snatched the pad of paper out of her hand. The chase was on! With a flying tackle, I wrestled him to the ground, while Sally pried the pad from his jaws.

Before anything else could happen, we headed back to town and sent off an order for the harnesses. I asked for three extras in varying sizes for new team members we might add. Then, with Solomon's words of harness-eating dogs in mind, I added two more to the order.

While we waited for the harnesses to arrive in the mail, Sally and I continued asking around for more dogs. We had a feeling we might need more than five dogs to haul a loaded toboggan on our upcoming journey. Now that mushers were starting to run their teams, we hoped they might decide that a dog or two wasn't cut out for racing. Sure enough, a musher approached us a few days later.

"My dog pulls hard, but he doesn't run fast enough for me," the musher said. "He didn't have puppies last year, so he is a strong dog."

I was confused. "Is he a male?" I asked.

I politely declined when he turned out to be a she. As we continued on our way, Sally and I chuckled at the ambiguity of translating Cree to English.

It was an exciting day for Sally and me when our harnesses and tug-lines arrived a week later. However, the dogs merely greeted us with yawns as we walked to the dog yard that morning. They had no real reason to be excited; supper didn't come till just before sunset.

Then I pulled the harnesses from a canvas bag. Five sleepy creatures were instantly transformed into howling sled dogs who couldn't wait to be out running.

"Apparently they know what this means," I said to Sally.

Jeff was slightly less hyperactive than the others, so we decided to harness him first. I turned a tangle of webbing over in my hands, getting it straight in my mind which part went where. Then I approached our leader.

"You hold him and I'll put on the harness," I said in a stage whisper.

While Jeff trembled with anticipation, I slipped the padded collar over his head. Gently, I lifted one front leg and guided it through a loop of webbing. As I repeated the procedure with his other leg, Sally stroked him behind the ears.

"That wasn't so tough," Sally said as I fastened the belly band.

"Right . . . nothing to it," I agreed. But we spoke too soon. Blue decided to play hard to catch, forcing us to chase him around and around his tree until Sally stepped on his chain and wrestled him to the snow. Then he jerked his foot away each time I tried to guide it into the harness. After a dozen repetitions, Blue grew tired of the game and we finally harnessed him.

Buck's reaction was the complete opposite. He rushed at me, shoving his head into the harness and knocking me into the snow. The next two dogs repeated Buck's performance, hardly able to contain their enthusiasm.

"Umm . . . you're stronger, so I think you should lead the dogs to the toboggan," Sally said after we had finished harnessing the team.

Without fully understanding the implications of the task ahead, I agreed. Confidently, I approached Jeff, slipping a hand under his collar and releasing his chain. The moment he heard the chain drop to the snow, he broke into a run towards the toboggan, dragging me behind.

"Look out!" I shouted as we almost bowled Sally over. I regained my footing just as we reached the toboggan, then wrestled Jeff to the front of the tug-lines. As I tried to keep him from squirming about, Sally clipped a tug-line to each side of his harness.

After being dragged to the toboggan by Tom, Buck, Hank, and Blue, I was sweating, even though the temperature was well below freezing.

"I'm tuckered out, and we haven't gone anywhere yet!" I declared, puffing loudly.

However, there was no time to rest. The dogs were accustomed to being attached to a single tug-line, not the old-fashioned double tug-lines we were using. By the time Blue was clipped in, every other dog was tangled in the two lines. Thankful that there were no spectators, we unclipped harnesses, untangled dogs, and wrestled with our excited team members.

I had no sooner straightened out the other dogs when Blue rolled onto his back to rub where the harness compressed his fur. How two pieces of rope could get twisted into such a tangle defied all laws of physics.

Finally, by holding Jeff at the front, Sally was able to keep the lines tight.

"Hold Jeff like that until I give the signal to go, then jump out of the way," I called. Before Sally could suggest an alternative, I ran to the back of the toboggan and released the snub rope from around a tree.

The moment I released the knot, the toboggan was launched into motion; I didn't even have a chance to call "Hike!" Five dogs almost ran Sally over in the excitement.

"Jump in!" I called. With a flying leap, Sally landed in the *carriole* bag.

For one full, exhilarating minute, the dogs ran straight ahead, snow flying from their feet.

Then, suddenly, Jeff stopped in his tracks. The other dogs piled into him, and instantly were ensnared by the tug-lines. Buck and Hank exchanged angry growls and started to fight.

"Hank!" I shouted angrily.

This must have sounded like "Hike!" because the dogs lurched ahead, pulling the toboggan with them. I gave the command to stop, and threw the snow hook into the snow.

My "Whoa!" had little effect, but luckily the curved, steel

Ian and Hank

Sally and Buck

Untangling the dogs

snow hook did. The dogs were almost jerked off their feet as the hook dug into the ground beneath the thin layer of snow.

Hank and Buck took this opportunity to resume their fight. Not wanting to miss out on the excitement, the others joined in with snarls and yelps. The front two dogs were completely tangled with the next two.

"No!" Sally called out, running to the team—a surprising reaction, considering her fear of snarling dogs. By the time I reached the team, Sally had managed to grab Hank's collar. But somehow, she had ended up with Tom's tug-lines wrapped tightly around her legs. Until Sally extricated herself, she could do nothing to help.

I ran into the fight, shouting loudly. Barks and shouts rose to a crescendo as I lunged at Buck and grabbed him by the scruff of his neck. Frantically, I unclipped his harness, dragged him away and tied him to the toboggan. As soon as I pulled off another dog, the fight was over.

"Poor Tom, he was just standing there and someone bit him," Sally said, wiping blood from his ear. Both she and Tom were trembling.

When everyone had calmed down, we decided to try again. Hank and Buck had been the instigators of the brawl, so we changed their positions in the team.

Once again, I called "Hike!" and the dogs leaped into motion. Three dogs ran straight ahead and two ran backwards.

As I stopped the team by dragging the snow hook, I realized our first training runs were going to require a lot of patience. It must have been difficult for the dogs as well. They were with people they were unfamiliar with and harnessed to paired tug-lines they had never seen before. In addition, they were hooked up to a large, lumbering toboggan instead of a light racing sled. I decided to try a different approach.

As if nothing had gone wrong, I petted every dog, taking time to praise them and rub them behind the ears.

"Come on, boys, you know what to do," I said gently.

This time, when I gave the command to go they all ran the same direction. We were making progress.

A few paces before the first turn, I glanced down to remind myself which letter I had carved on the right handlebar. Then I called Jeff's name and said "Gee" to signal a right turn. We went roaring past the turn, veering left.

"Whoa," I called, digging in the snow hook.

Sally jumped out of the toboggan, herded the dogs in the correct direction, then we set off again.

We finished our run after half an hour, pleased that we made it back to the dog yard without any more fights or pile-ups. The dogs were equally pleased with the outing, judging by their wagging tails.

The dogs were as eager as ever the next day, leaping against their lines and barking loudly when I pulled out the harnesses. After another rowdy hook-up, I released the snub rope and the dogs shot forward, leaving Sally to jump onto the toboggan as it sped by. Our blast-off needed work, but we were on our way!

Just before reaching the first turn, Jeff stopped running, and we had another pile-up. He stood with his tail between his legs and looked back at me, as if not sure what to expect.

"At least they're not fighting," Sally said as we untangled dogs from the lines.

"I kind of liked the excitement," I replied. Sally looked at me in surprise, then laughed. She knew as well as I that we could do without that kind of excitement.

Sally coaxed the team around the corner while I gave the "Gee" command, then she leaped onto the toboggan as it slid past.

At the next turn, I stopped the team before Jeff had a chance to cause a pile-up. Sally led Jeff the correct way while I called the appropriate command. Several turns later, Jeff seemed to be gaining more confidence.

The run was as exasperating as it was exciting. I just started to relax when Blue somehow stepped over a tug-line

Our team ready to go

All running in one direction

and began loping on three legs. Grumbling under my breath, I stopped the team, untangled Blue, and then we started off again. The toboggan had barely reached cruising speed when Tom slowed to relieve himself. The others, still running, crashed into him.

"Let's aim for a hundred paces this time!" I said to Sally as we untangled the dogs again. Half an hour and two tangles later, we made it back to the dog yard.

Over the next days we kept a log of where we put each dog and details about the run. Tangles became fewer and the dogs seemed to be getting used to their team-mates. Sally and I were learning to match their personalities and preferences for running positions.

Even so, there was something new to deal with every day. Hank often lay down and refused to run until we coaxed and petted him. Blue had a habit of running on the outside of the two tug-lines instead of between them. And Buck still growled at other dogs during tangles, although a swat on his nose each time was slowly curing him of that habit.

The dogs were performing better with each run, but we were still having trouble with our leader. Just when we thought Jeff was working out, he decided he didn't want the responsibility of leading by himself. Several times during each outing he would drop back to run with the dog directly behind him. As a result both dogs became tangled in the slack lines.

We tried Hank and then Buck as leaders, but they refused to run when I gave the command to go. Blue led the team on a merry chase through bushes, across an open field, then over a fallen tree until the toboggan thudded to a stop. We even considered putting Tom up front.

"We must be getting desperate," I remarked. "Can you imagine having a one-eyed dog as a leader?"

It was time to visit other mushers for advice. Our best source of encouragement came from Clifford Carrière, who had used dogs on his trap line until a few years ago. Unlike most mushers who ran their dogs as racing teams, he was familiar with the old way of travelling.

When Sally told him of our troubles with Jeff, Clifford suggested that we were being too lenient.

"You just have to let them know who the boss is. It's dangerous to have them disobey you out on the trail," Clifford said.

He told us about one of his leaders who turned for home three times. Three times Clifford stopped the team, turned the dog around, and continued.

"After that I had no more problems. You have to win the battle each time," he concluded.

Perhaps we had been too gentle with Jeff. On the next runs I reprimanded him when he stopped without my command, and praised him each time he made a correct turn. My journal entry for December 15 summed up our progress: "Best run yet! The dogs are pulling hard and running in the same direction." Jeff still dropped back and tangled the team at the worst possible times, but with lots of training, I hoped he would work out.

Over the next days, we travelled farther and added sandbags to the toboggan to simulate the load we would carry on our journey. However, by the time we increased the weight to more than one hundred pounds of sand, it became apparent that we didn't have enough pulling power.

The few dogs that were available locally were not strong enough to pull a load or did not have enough fur to sleep in the snow at night. The best one we could find was smaller than Tom, but he had a bark that irritated the other dogs and us. Still, we were hopeful—until we discovered that he had a penchant for chewing through the tug-lines. After he'd chewed the third one, we realized that he would be a serious liability on a long trip. We returned him to his owner.

Next we tried a dog named Brownie. His owner wasn't sure how he would work and offered to let us try him with our team for a few days. He was a fat, husky breed, not yet fully grown in stature or mind, judging by his puppy-like antics. When we hooked him up he ran, but only enough to avoid being dragged along by the tug-lines.

We spent several days working with him, but came to the conclusion he didn't want to pull. The desire to pull is the most important trait in a sled dog and Brownie just didn't have it. Sally and I went to visit his owner.

"How many times has Brownie run this season?" I asked, thinking that perhaps Brownie was merely out of shape.

"Only once," he answered. That explained Brownie's slow pace.

"What about last season? He doesn't really want to pull," I said.

"I never ran him before last week. He was my father's pet and ran loose until a few months ago."

I looked at Sally; her eyes showed she could barely contain her laughter. With as much tact as possible, I gave Brownie back.

Sally and I continued training our team of five. Although they were becoming stronger every day, we wondered how they would manage hauling a loaded toboggan through deep snow during our planned six-week journey. We visited Clifford again to see if he had any ideas about where we might find more dogs.

"Maybe you'll find some at the New Year's race. There will be many teams there," Clifford suggested.

That was it! We would hound the mushers after the race and try to round up a couple more dogs. Meanwhile, we would keep training our team and enjoy the coming week of winter celebrations.

FOURTEEN

Winter Celebrations

"I'll just drop by the North West Company to see if they have any dog chain," I announced after a training run with the team. Sally smiled knowingly and nodded. It was nearing Christmas, and I needed an excuse to go to the store by myself.

While shopping, I stopped at the back counter to read Arnold a quote from Alexander Henry's journal about Christmas in Cumberland House: "This being the Christmas season, agreeably to the custom of the country, the factor of the fort treated his people with High Wines, Flour and Sugar. There was much excitement among the men, as provisions had been wanting for some time."

"Are ye hinting at something, laddie?" Arnold asked, his eyes twinkling. He paused for a moment, then asked if Sally and I would like to join him and Rita for Christmas dinner.

"What a pleasant surprise . . . we'd love to!" I replied.

On Christmas Day we made our way to Arnold and Rita's house through a swirling snowstorm. We talked of years gone by and celebrations they had shared in different posts across the north. Then we exchanged presents of heavy socks, scarves, and mitts. With the thermometer hovering at thirty below outside, we appreciated these practical gifts more than any fancy presents we'd received other years. And the wool socks were a perfect accessory for the long johns I had given Sally that morning. I knew the five large ham bones donated by the store would be equally appreciated by our dogs.

Rita cooked a traditional turkey dinner with all the trimmings. For dessert, we savoured home-cooked plum pudding with rum sauce along with shortbread cookies and other baked treats. It was a sumptuous feast.

"Merry Christmas to all," Arnold said, proposing a toast.

"Does that include your competitors too?" I prodded after the toast. "I read that during the fur trade, the rivalry between companies was suspended this time of year—the Nor'Westers even invited the Hudson's Bay Company factors and clerks to join the feast."

Rita suppressed a smile. I was well known for spouting on the topic of the fur traders.

"Why don't you go round up some Bay men for a bit of plum pudding?" she asked, pointing to the door. Everyone laughed.

Between Christmas visits, Sally and I continued our training runs with the dogs. Jeff was still a reluctant leader, sometimes turning for home when he became over-whelmed with the responsibility. The team still struggled to pull the toboggan-load of sandbags, but we were making progress.

The December days were short and cold. By the time we had harnessed the dogs, run them for an hour or so, then unharnessed each dog and fed them, it was usually dark. We looked forward to the daylight hours growing longer in the new year.

Sally and I celebrated New Year's Eve with Clifford and Lily Carrière. Chilled after feeding the dogs, we stepped into their house and were greeted with the warmth and noise of a party underway. We inhaled a medley of scents— from wet wool clothing to hot apple cider, bannock, and whitefish. Laughter echoed throughout the house as children chased each other from room to room.

Among the adults there was a great deal of talk about the King and Queen Trapper contests as well as the dog races that would take place the following day.

"Queen Trapper?" Sally asked, her competitive nature rising to the surface.

With a mischievous grin, Clifford handed Sally a list of the skills that would be tested.

"I'll try the moose call," Sally said gamely after scanning the list. Clifford handed her a megaphone-shaped roll of birchbark.

Taking a deep breath, Sally grunted into the horn. The subsequent silence spoke volumes!

"Guess moose speak a different language where I come from!" she announced with a grin.

"Ha! You weren't *calling* a moose. That was a grunt of a moose running away," Clifford said. "In the contest you have to say what you're doing, like 'This is the challenge call of a bull' or 'This is a cow calling for a mate.' "

"Okay, this is a calf," Sally said.

With one hand pinching her nose and the other hand covering the end of the horn, she made a wailing sound that sounded more like an alley cat than a moose. When the laughter died down, Clifford coached Sally again.

"Try a bull moose . . . you make a breathing sound like someone working hard," he said. When Sally tried the call everyone roared with laughter at the sensual overtones she produced.

Sally hadn't realized the tough competition she would be up against until Clifford's twelve-year-old daughter, Mika, mimicked the call of a goose far away then close, calling faster as it circled overhead.

"That was so convincing, I almost looked up," Sally said. "By the way, what types of geese are found here?"

"Canada, snow, and blue geese," someone stated.

"No brants, eh?" Sally said, realizing that they would probably be unfamiliar with this coastal bird. "That's what I'll do!"

The evening went quickly, and suddenly it was nearing midnight. There was great anticipation as everyone who had brought a shotgun went outside. This was an event we'd been hearing about for weeks.

"Look out the window," Lily announced to all the children. "They're going to shoot the Devil!"

The lights were dimmed and children rushed to press their noses to the window. Throughout Cumberland House, shotguns were fired into the air. The staccato report of guns echoed through the still night. Shots continued long after midnight, depending on how people's watches were set or how much ammunition was available.

We learned that this custom of "shooting the Devil" to start a new year had been performed for as long as anyone could remember. Even Alexander Henry had written about the new year being ushered in by volleys of gunshot.

A thick cloud of cold mist billowed in along the floor as each person came into the house. Wreathed in frost and smiles, the noise-makers removed their coats and piled them by the door.

While people warmed their hands over the woodburning stove, Lily laid out a New Year's feast of roast duck, wild rice, fresh bannock, squash, and endless other goodies. My favourite part of the meal was the dessert, called putchin. This pudding, boiled in a canvas bag, is a blend of flour, Saskatoon berries, raisins, and spices.

"Too bad putchin eating isn't part of the King Trapper contest. You'd be the winner," Lily teased as I helped myself to another piece. At two in the morning, Sally and I rolled home.

The New Year's Day events began at noon with dog races. Several teams from around Saskatchewan and Manitoba arrived, and the village was alive with scores of dogs howling and barking. The excitement grew as teams began to line up at a starting line scraped in the snow. Dogs barked frantically and lunged against their harnesses, hoping to break the sleds free from whatever was restraining them.

"Glad to see our hook-ups aren't unusual," Sally commented when she saw a team become hopelessly tangled at the starting line.

Spectators were asked to hold dogs, untangle lines, and unclip harnesses. Finally, all was sorted out. By the time ten teams were assembled, the din was deafening.

At the sharp retort of a gunshot they were off—a blur of paws, whirr of runners, and encouraging shouts from the mushers. Minutes after the dogs had left, all was quiet.

Sally and I shuffled about with the other spectators, stamping our feet to keep warm in the minus-thirty degree temperature while we waited for the return of the teams. Half an hour later, the first dogs crossed the finish line to the muffled clapping of mittened hands.

At the end of the race, all mushers had a story to tell. "The curve" had claimed its toll of toques and hats, and several mushers had slid into the bushes on the fast turn. Others told of tangles, dog fights, snow hooks coming out, and assorted tales to explain why their team hadn't come first this day. Every musher wore a broad smile and had a team of happy dogs.

"Ready for the Queen Trapper events?" Clifford asked Sally when the dog races were over.

"I think I'll just watch and learn this time," Sally replied.

When we arrived at the competition site, several people were preparing their bow saws for the wood-sawing contest. Some saws were rusty; others had been carefully removed from protective canvas covers and coated with a film of oil. Men and women competed at the same time, although there were separate judges for the King and Queen Trappers. This was a serious event with a large purse going to the winners that night.

The competitor with the oiled saw won the contest several minutes ahead of those using rusty or blunt saws. During the nail-hammering and axe-throwing contests Sally was thinking that she should have entered the competition.

As we watched the snowshoe race, Sally reconsidered.

"I don't think I would have done very well, after all," she conceded as several women sprinted across the hard-packed snow on snowshoes that were half the size of Sally's.

Still puffing from the snowshoe races, the contestants began to prepare for the tea-boiling contest. Each person jammed a pole into the snowbank and hung a tea pail in readiness. The pots, blackened from previous fires, were filled to the top with snow. After selecting a round of wood, everyone stood poised at their pail, axe in hand.

At the signal to start, the quiet air turned into a frenzy of eleven axes chopping the blocks of wood. Within a couple of minutes some blocks had been split into kindling and piled around the tea pails.

Each contestant had six matches to light a fire. The most skilled lit theirs with only one; others ran out of matches and had to quit.

"Boiling!" someone called eight minutes later. The call was repeated from one direction then another, keeping the judges busy.

"Eight minutes! Think you can beat that out on the trail?" Sally asked, as we warmed ourselves by one of the fires.

"Of course . . . even with a flint and steel in a snowstorm," I boasted. Secretly, I wondered how efficient Sally and I would be when making tea on our journey.

As darkness descended over the village, everyone wandered over to the community hall. The next event was leg wrestling. To our surprise, the smaller men and women were often the winners. Here, technique seemed to be more important than strength or size. A slim woman easily pulled over a much larger opponent with a quick twist of her hips.

"Wish I'd seen that before wrestling with Hal last summer," I said to Sally. Her response was doused by the roar of the audience cheering the winner.

Finally, the event Sally had been waiting for was announced—the animal calls. First up was a teenage girl to do a "spring goose arriving." She cupped fingers over her mouth, calling softly, her call growing louder and louder, then fading away as she simulated a goose landing. Another woman mimicked a mallard feeding, then a warning call. They certainly sounded like mallards to me. Sally's moose call wouldn't have had a chance!

For us, the best part of the New Year's activities was meeting dog musher John Calvert, who was visiting from The Pas. We joined the group of mushers where he was sharing stories of past races. I chuckled when someone called him Grandpa.

"Some guys think I'm too old for this," he said to Sally and me later. "But it doesn't matter . . . I've got young dogs!"

Over coffee, we told him of our plans to follow the trails that voyageurs had taken from post to post. When his interest peaked, I mentioned that we still needed more dogs.

"I have one good puller you could buy," John said. I agreed to the price he named, then asked if he knew anyone with a leader for sale.

"I have a good leader who's a bit slow for racing. But he's not for sale."

John thought for a long moment, studying me. "Tell you what. I'll lend him to you," he said.

I was overwhelmed that someone we'd just met would lend us a lead dog. Sally and I thanked John profusely for his generous offer. With two more dogs for our team, our winter journey was now possible.

"Somehow, I knew things would work out," I said to Sally as we walked home. Even so, I was still amazed that, once again, we had met the right person at the right time.

Sally and I were so eager to meet our new dogs that we barely slept that night. With considerable restraint, we waited till after sunrise to arrive at John's house in The Pas.

John introduced us to Sting, a handsome brown and white husky. Although he was shy of Sally and me, he had the proud stance of a dog who was obviously a leader. The other dog was named Link. He was young, with floppy ears and jet-black fur from head to foot.

Jeff

Tom

Blue

Hank

178

Buck   *Link*

Sting

179

"You'll never lose this one in a snowstorm," John said, ruffling Link's fur. Both Link and Sting met our exacting standards for sled dogs—their tails wagged and they didn't bite.

After giving Sting and Link a few days to become familiar with their new team-mates, we decided to take all the dogs for a run. The din in the dog yard at hook-up was almost deafening. Now, seven dogs yapped and howled and barked in anticipation. If the noise was any indication of pulling power, we were in for quite a ride.

Sting was still timid, and I had to coax him to the lead position of the tug-lines. With the tug-lines extended to accommodate two more dogs, Sting was almost fifty feet from where I would stand at the rear of the toboggan. I wondered if he would hear my commands over the noise of the other dogs.

Sally stroked Sting behind the ears to calm him while I started hooking up the other dogs. When Sally came to help me with Buck, Sting remained out front, holding the lines tight. We were impressed that he remained there unattended—it was quite a feat with the other dogs pulling the lines left and right as they jumped around.

"This looks promising," I said as I hooked up the last dog.

Still unsure of how our blast-off would go, I nodded to Sally. Warily, she walked towards the toboggan.

As soon as Sally had settled in the *carriole*, I released the snub rope and called "Hike!"

Sting leaped into his harness as if prodded from behind. The other dogs followed his lead, running flat out. It was all we could do to hang on to the speeding toboggan. As we raced down the trail, trees flashed by like a picket fence. Sally gave me a thumbs-up signal, and I knew that behind the scarf covering her face, she was grinning as broadly as I was. I only hoped Sting would stop as efficiently as he had started.

It was surprising the difference two additional dogs made. The team usually slowed after the first ten-minute sprint, but now they kept running at a full lope, tongues lolling from their mouths and twenty-eight paws flying over the snow.

At the first sharp turn, the toboggan slewed around the corner and bounced against a snowbank. We had never taken the corner at this speed before and I hung on with all my strength. I remembered the first rule of mushing: stay with the sled under all circumstances.

Sally was having an equally wild ride at the front of the toboggan. She lurched forward with each bump in the trail, arms straining against ropes that she gripped in mittened hands. When we hit the snowbank, I thought she was going to be catapulted from the toboggan. Next run we would add more weight to slow the dogs down. After all, our goal was to have them pull freight, not compete in a race!

Because this was Sting's first outing with me as his new master, I wasn't surprised when he tested me by turning off the trail without a command. Each time he did this, Sally led him in the correct direction and then we continued down the trail. Gently, but persistently, I affirmed my position as Sting's master and gave directions at each turn. After an hour with few mishaps, we returned to the yard feeling pleased with our first run with a team of seven dogs.

"That was great!" Sally said, smiling broadly as we unhooked the panting dogs.

Sting was last to be unhooked and stood proudly, tail high and ears perked up. To our relief, Jeff didn't seem upset at having been demoted to a team dog. In fact, he had pulled harder with dogs in front of him than he ever had as a leader.

With each training run, the dogs began to work better as a team. Tangles became fewer, and dogfights were a rare event. Best of all, after a lot of petting and perseverance, Sting was beginning to accept me as his new master. He now obeyed my commands at almost every turn.

To prepare the dogs for our upcoming journey, we added more weight to the toboggan every few days. We trained in snowstorms, on icy trails, and even when the temperature dipped below minus thirty. The dogs needed to become accustomed to working in all conditions, and we needed to test the effectiveness of our clothing and equipment. It was easier to make repairs and adjustments now than it would be on the trail in a cold tent.

Between outings we modified our clothing, reinforced harnesses, and braided spare tug-lines. While Sally sewed canvas bags for the dog chains and other gear, I made two wooden boxes to hold our food and cooking equipment.

By late January, Sally and I had been working with all seven dogs for almost a month. They were now able to pull a toboggan-load of sandbags at a fast trot for almost two hours without tiring. We were ready to go camping with the team. At least, we thought we were ready.

FIFTEEN

Toboggan Trails

I heaved two canvas bags of dog food onto the toboggan, then the wooden boxes containing our food, pots, and loose items. By the time we added the heavy canvas tent, bulky clothing, and other supplies, the *carriole* bag was bulging at the seams.

Although we were going on just a four-day training run, we packed all the food and equipment required for a longer journey. Our goal was to see how the dogs managed with the fully loaded toboggan.

After tying in the load, Sally and I put our weight behind the toboggan to push it to the dog yard. It hardly budged.

"Yikes! It feels like the snub rope is still tied to a tree," Sally exclaimed. We estimated that the loaded toboggan, with our camping gear and supplies, weighed more than three hundred pounds. It took all of our strength to move it fifty paces.

Our combined weight with heavy winter clothes would add another three hundred pounds to the load. Neither of us dared express the thought that the dogs might not be able to move the toboggan.

"Umm, let's not tell the dogs," Sally joked as we

approached them with harnesses in hand.

"Okay, boys, you're in for a treat today!" I announced cheerfully. They responded with their usual enthusiasm, jumping and barking loudly. The wonderful thing about working with dogs was that they were always happy to see us. It wasn't long before their exuberance banished our doubts.

"Ready?" I asked Sally. The dogs were definitely ready. Each one leaped impatiently against the tug-lines. Sally walked back to the toboggan, double-checking the harness of each dog on her way. As Sally and I pushed the toboggan to break it loose from the snow, I urged the dogs ahead.

"Hike!"

Each dog clawed at the snow, straining against the unusually heavy load. To our amazement, the dogs pulled eagerly, although Buck and Blue looked back to see why they weren't able to run as fast as usual. I ran behind, pushing on the handles to give the toboggan momentum. Once we were moving, Sally jumped on top of the load.

At the first corner, the weight of the loaded toboggan sent it veering off the trail. In slow motion, it began to tip over. As Sally tumbled into the soft snow, the toboggan rolled on top of her. All three hundred pounds of it.

"Are you okay?" I called, skidding to my knees at the snowbank's edge.

"Mmph," came the muffled reply from under the toboggan. A moment later her head emerged from the snowbank.

"I think I'd rather be on the toboggan than under it!" she said, sputtering. "Get this thing off me, will you?"

I put my shoulder into the load, attempting to right the toboggan without stepping on Sally. As the tug-lines jerked backwards, seven stalled dogs turned to see what was happening.

"Stay! Stay!" I shouted. The last thing I wanted was for the dogs to come to the toboggan and get tangled in the lines. Luckily, they didn't seem inclined to join us. I suppose the sight of their intrepid masters grovelling in the snow did not inspire great confidence.

"Good boys," I praised. But as soon as the dogs heard the toboggan thump onto the trail, they were off and running. Sally and I scrambled after the toboggan and jumped on.

The loaded toboggan handled much differently than it had on training runs when weighed down with only a few sandbags. Several turns later, I learned to pull sideways on the handlebars to pivot the toboggan well ahead of each corner. We managed to get around the next corners without going off the trail, but it would take a lot of practice to handle the toboggan with confidence.

Just as I was catching my breath, the dogs slowed to a walk at an uphill stretch of the trail. Sally got off the toboggan to lighten the load, while I pushed on the handlebars. When the trail levelled off, the dogs sped up to a trot again, surprisingly tolerant of the heavy weight behind them.

My worry that they might refuse to pull the loaded toboggan was unfounded. These dogs loved to be on the trail!

"Good boys!" I called. Fourteen ears perked up at the encouraging tone of my voice.

By mid-afternoon Sally and I began to look for a campsite. The dogs were slowing noticeably after three hours of travel, and we felt it best not to overwork them on our first day. Also, we needed plenty of time to set up camp and feed the dogs before the sun dropped below the horizon.

"That looks good," Sally said, pointing to a small clearing in the forest. Our requirements were minimal: a sheltered place for the tent and a clear area large enough for the dogs.

While Sally remained at the toboggan, holding the team, I secured a long stake-out chain between two trees.

"Whoa, whoa," I heard Sally call out again and again. The dogs, having no idea this was the end of the run for the day, impatiently lunged against the lines.

One by one, I led the dogs to the stake-out area I had stamped in the snow with my snowshoes. Back at the dog yard they had each been tied to a separate tree, but now the dogs were all attached to one long chain. Each dog had enough room to move around but not enough to tangle with his neighbours.

It appeared that the dogs had never been camping before. They were unsure of the situation, sniffing at the dogs beside them and pawing at the snow. As well, they pranced in circles, jumped back and forth over the chain or squeezed under it, sometimes becoming stuck halfway.

Sally brought the dogs some bedding of spruce boughs, which they eagerly anticipated as she approached. One by one, their tails stopped wagging when they inspected their beds. Compared to the soft straw they were accustomed to, this was definitely second-rate.

We watched Blue circle a dozen times, then tentatively sit down. A millisecond later, he leaped up as sharp spruce needles penetrated his thin fur. Again and again, he repeated this performance. Buck, on the other hand, was under the impression his bed might be edible and spent the first few minutes gnawing on the branches. Hank shunned his bed entirely and curled up in the snow.

Tom remained standing. With sad eyes he looked at Sally, then at the boughs.

"I feel guilty, knowing we have soft wool blankets," Sally said as she fluffed up Tom's prickly bed.

"Come on, Tom," she coaxed, patting the bed. Finally he lay down, seeming to understand that spruce boughs were better than nothing. The others continued to sniff and paw at their beds.

"Don't look at them, Sal . . . we have to set up camp," I pleaded. I had visions of her spending the evening tucking each dog into bed.

As Sally and I continued our camp chores, seven pairs of eyes watched our every move. Sally stamped down an area with her snowshoes to make a platform for the tent while I gathered firewood. While waiting for the compressed snow to harden, I lit a fire and hung pots of snow above the flames.

"Where are the tent pegs?" Sally called out, rifling through a canvas bag at the toboggan.

Taking a break

Setting up camp

"I think they're in the grub box," I replied. I knew they were on the toboggan somewhere—after all, we had used a checklist to ensure we packed everything. It would take a few nights to get our camping routine sorted out. Luckily the temperature was only twenty below; when it became colder we would need to be more efficient.

Half an hour later, we had the tent set up and the pots of snow had melted to water. As I pulled out the feeding bowls for the dogs, they perked up at the familiar sound of clinking metal. Each dog lunged against the chain in anticipation.

"We'd better feed the dogs next . . . they'll drive us crazy with their barking," Sally said. We poured dog food into two large pots of water and set them aside to soak. The dogs snapped to attention each time we stirred the food or even lifted a lid.

The barking rose to a crescendo when I gave Sting his supper. By feeding him first, I reaffirmed his status as lead dog. The others followed in order of their position during hook-up. Link drooled on my trousers and Buck leaped up, almost knocking me over. Blue snatched his bowl out of my hand.

"This is like running the gauntlet," I said as I carried the next bowl down the line. Finally, the only sound was the slurping of food being devoured by seven hungry dogs.

By the time we began to cook our own supper, the sun had dipped below the treetops. Soon, steam was rising from the pot and our damp mitts and moccasins hanging over the fire. Back in Cumberland House, we had taken for granted that our clothes would be dry each morning. Now we had to spend the evening turning each item and watching for stray sparks.

It was a pleasant task though, sitting outside on this quiet, windless night. The campfire lit up the trees with an orange glow and cast weird shadows upon the tent and surrounding bushes. Bright sparks spiralled into the black night.

When supper was ready, Sally and I wolfed our meal

down almost as fast as the dogs had eaten theirs.

"You'd fit right in with the roughest crew of voyageurs," Sally said, and laughed. My priority was to eat my food before it congealed on the plate.

"What do you mean?" I asked, then saw the clumsy way I was gripping my spoon with a mittened fist.

"Well, I suppose etiquette takes back seat to practicality," I conceded. With an exaggerated gesture, Sally tossed the dregs of her tea over a shoulder. I flicked a pine needle from my supper into the fire, where it sizzled aromatically.

"I'll do the dishes," I offered after supper, picking up the pot and plates. With a scoop of granular snow, I scrubbed the tinware before the remnants of supper could freeze to the bottom.

Then I filled the pot with fresh snow to melt for water. I would have to fill the pot with snow two or three more times to yield a full pot of water. Breakfast would have a mild taste of the pea soup we'd had for supper, but that was just part of winter camping.

The dogs continued to watch our activities, barking now and then when we spoke or when I lifted a pot lid. They turned, sat, then stood to watch us. They turned again and sat down, not quite sure what was happening. Only after dark did the dogs become convinced we weren't taking them home to a nice bed of straw. One by one, they curled up on their spruce-bough beds.

"I think they've got the right idea," Sally said, yawning. We were both tired from our first day of travel, and made our way to the tent by the last light of the fire.

By the time I'd passed blanket coats, moccasins, wool leggings, and other gear to Sally in the tent, there was little room to move. I crouched at the door while Sally hung our moccasins along the ridge of the tent, then spread our *capotes* over the blankets for extra insulation.

"Comfy yet?" I asked a bit impatiently, as Sally fussed over her bedding almost as much as the dogs had.

"Okay, okay, I'm finished," she said finally, when she had tucked herself in.

I crawled into the tent, careful not to punch knee-holes in the snow beneath the tarp we slept on. Then I settled into bed with slightly damp socks wedged between the blankets and with a pillow of rolled-up trousers under my head.

The dogs were restless and woke us frequently with their barking. During the darkest, coldest hour of the night, we woke to the sound of the dogs howling, seven distinct voices echoing through the forest.

"What now?" Sally mumbled.

"Listen!" Not far away, came the response of wolves howling. More voices joined in, starting on a high note, then slowly dropping in tone and volume.

Ow, ow, owwhoo-oo-oo. The wavering howls became louder and more intense as the wolves drew closer. It was eerie and wonderful to hear this call, so timeless and wild. Our team replied with a harmony that reverberated in the still night air.

Sally and I woke again just as diffused daylight illuminated the tent. We soon discovered why wedge tents are no longer used—it was so cramped only one of us could sit up at a time. Being a gentleman, and reluctant to rise from my cozy sleeping robe, I offered to let Sally dress first.

"Ahh!" she groaned loudly, as a shower of frost from the wall sifted down her neck.

"Quiet, you'll wake the dogs," I said, stifling a laugh. After having been awake for much of the night, they no doubt planned to sleep in.

Sally dressed quickly, considering the contortions she had to perform. While lying down, she wriggled into wool long-john top and bottoms. As she pulled on her trousers, she bumped into the tent wall again.

"Get off my stomach," I complained when Sally ducked away from the falling frost.

"I will if you move over!" she said, pushing me towards the wall of frost. To avoid a repeat performance, I shifted aside until my nose nearly touched the sloping roof. By the time Sally had added her bulky wool *capote*, she was definitely taking up more than her share of the tent. I diplomatically suggested that she lace up her moccasins outside.

When I emerged from the tent, Sally was already lighting a fire. I went to the toboggan to dig out a sack of oatmeal.

"Sally, look at this!" I called. Fresh wolf tracks led along the trail between the toboggan and the dogs.

"No wonder the dogs were so restless," Sally said. There were several sets of tracks, with one set detouring towards the team, then back to the trail. That wolf must have caused the commotion that woke us.

Seven snoozing creatures came to life at the sound of our voices. Even though we fed them only once a day, they watched expectantly, probably hoping for extra rations. Each time I stirred the oatmeal, Link and Buck barked. I felt a pang of guilt eating breakfast in front of the ever-hungry dogs. They watched us intently as we packed up camp, and when I picked up the dog pots, the team went berserk.

"Having a nice, peaceful morning in the wilderness?" I called to Sally. Her answer was lost among the barks reverberating through the forest.

When we approached the dogs with harnesses in hand, they wriggled like happy puppies. We said hello to each one, then began to harness them.

Hooking the dogs to the toboggan was not much different than it had been back at the dog yard. However, it was all Sally could do to hold them while I untied the stake-out chain. They leaped, they howled, they clawed at the snow. Until now, we had always blasted off as soon as the last dog was hooked up. This time, they had to wait until the chain was packed away.

"Hurry up, Ian," Sally urged. The rope holding the toboggan to a tree jerked each time the dogs lunged forward. I had visions of my knot coming undone, and the team running down the trail, never to be seen again.

I ran to the toboggan and threw the chain aboard. The moment I released the snub rope, we were off!

Shortly after we began, the trail dropped onto the white,

open expanse of a lake. Sting ran two paces onto the feature-less lake, then stopped in his tracks. The stop was so sudden and unexpected the dogs piled into him before I could throw in the snow hook.

"Whoa!" I called rather belatedly to the team. I stamped the hook into the snow and rushed forward to sort out the mess.

"Sacré morte chiens," I muttered in frustration. This voya-geur phrase, meaning "cursed dead dogs," had amused me when I read it months earlier. Now I said it with as much gusto as the roughest Northman.

We set off again, with the same results—a pile of dogs and tangled lines.

"Some leader!" Sally said.

"Me or Sting?" I shot back. Tactfully, she left the question unanswered.

It seemed that, without a trail to follow, Sting had no idea which way to go. The only solution we could think of was to make a trail. While I held the team, Sally started to snowshoe a path across the lake.

When Sally was part way across, I released the snow hook to let the dogs catch up to her. Sting promptly turned for the trail behind us, followed by the rest of the team. I struggled with a tangle of dogs and harnesses as Sting sat trembling, his tail between his legs.

Even with the snowshoe trail, he refused to move across the open expanse of the lake. I coaxed, then threatened Sting for almost ten minutes until Sally turned back to help, puffing after a long run.

"What's the matter?" she asked.

"Sting won't lead," I answered, tugging on his collar. He stood with legs locked, whining loudly.

We hadn't anticipated this sort of problem. However, it now dawned on me that Sting may never have been off a packed trail in his career as a racing dog.

"Any ideas?" I asked Sally.

"Well . . . didn't John Carrière say that Jeff was trained to follow someone on snowshoes?" she replied, after a bit of thought.

We traded the two dogs and to our relief, Jeff readily followed Sally across the lake. But as soon as Sally got onto the toboggan at the other side, Jeff pulled his old stunt of dropping back to be with the dog behind him.

I laughed out loud, not sure if I was exasperated or amused. In a way, I enjoyed the challenge of solving each problem as it came along. After all, new challenges were one reason we were here. We returned Sting to the lead position and he leaned into the harness, ready to pull again. Changing dogs mid-journey wasn't ideal, but by alternating leaders it appeared we would be able to go almost anywhere.

The trail we were following had been used since voyageur days as a route between posts and as a trapping trail. Now, few people came this way and much of the trail was just wide enough for our toboggan. Sally and I ducked and dodged and cursed the overhanging branches that slapped our faces. Clumps of snow fell off swaying branches, dropping neatly down the neck of my *capote*. Meanwhile, the dogs trotted merrily through the forest, oblivious of the plight of their passengers.

On the next twisting section of the trail, Sally and I were kept busy steering the toboggan around each corner. Kneeling at the front of the toboggan, Sally leaned left, then right, as she pulled against the snub rope. I heaved on the handlebars or dragged a foot to control my end. And Hank did his part as the "load dog" nearest the toboggan by leaning into the tug-lines to steer around each corner.

Just as I was congratulating Sally on our improved steering skills, we rounded a bend and saw a spruce tree leaning over the trail. The snow-laden branches just cleared the dogs' backs and Sally ducked, warding the tree off with one arm.

"Ummph!" was all I heard as Sally was swept off the front of the toboggan. Before I could duck, the branch sprang back towards me.

"Aargh!" I called as it struck me across the chest. I flew off the toboggan, joining Sally in the snowbank.

Spurred on by the shouts, the dogs continued at an increased clip, pulling a considerably lighter toboggan. I scrambled to my feet and sprinted after them.

"Whoa!" I called desperately, when I realized they were quickly outpacing me.

Fortunately, the dogs stopped at my command. Unfortunately, the loaded toboggan didn't. Three hundred pounds of cargo hurtled towards Hank. At the last possible moment he scrambled to one side, and I managed to grab the handlebars before the toboggan could plow into the next dog.

I ran up to the team, expecting to find tangled dogs, ready to fight as they had on our first runs. Instead, they turned to look at me, with canine smiles and tails wagging. They were having a great time!

"What a bunch of crazy dogs!" I said, laughing out loud. I rubbed Sting behind the ears, then patted and praised each of the others. Sally joined me, fussing over the dogs. In high spirits, we continued down the trail.

When we arrived at the next lake, we stopped and exchanged Jeff with Sting. While I held the team, Sally snowshoed ahead as she had on the previous lake.

Our system worked well enough, except I had difficulty holding the dogs back while they watched Sally snowshoe farther and farther away. As the dogs became impatient, they lunged against their harnesses, often pulling the hook from the snow. I let them catch up with Sally, then attempted to hold them back again.

At the third stop, I remembered that Clifford had suggested turning the toboggan on its side to keep it from freezing to the snow in warmer weather. Why not try that now to hold the dogs? With great effort, I heaved the toboggan over. It didn't take long for the dogs to realize it was impossible to move the dead weight. A couple of them even lay down until I flipped the toboggan upright again. When the toboggan thumped onto the snow, the dogs sprang to action, eager to catch up with Sally.

That evening we camped in a thick grove of spruce. The

Jeff leading across Belanger Lake

A four-legged tent warmer

dogs were not as restless as they had been on our first night, although they were still unimpressed by their spruce-bough beds. Once again, Hank chose to curl up in the snow. The others grudgingly lay on their beds after some fussing.

After another two days of travel, we returned to Cumberland House. I wasn't sure whether we had trained the dogs or they had trained us, but we had all learned a lot along the way.

Sally and I planned to stay in Cumberland House just long enough to mend harnesses and tug-lines and other equipment. Then we would pack supplies for a long journey. Now that we knew the dogs were able to pull a fully loaded toboggan, we were eager to explore new country.

Our inspiration came from a quote in Alexander Henry's Cumberland House journal: "The time has come to travel while the oatmeal-eaters tarry at their fort. To this end, I have chosen a train of stout dogs to pull a toboggan of trade goods. We are eager to proceed and the dogs are baying at their tethers."

Maps in hand, we visited Clifford to determine which trails would lead us to The Pas, Sturgeon Landing, Cranberry Portage, and beyond. The area around Cumberland House was flat and featureless, and our maps showed few details other than creeks, lakes, and rivers. The greater part of each sheet was coloured light green, translating to "lowland" on the map legend.

To Clifford, the maps told much more. He had trapped in the area for years and knew where the good camping spots were, which dark green area on each map was spruce forest and which was poplar.

Taking his time, Clifford drew all the routes he was familiar with onto our map, considering each line carefully. An *X* indicated where to avoid thin ice or where to detour around a beaver lodge. Each pencilled-in square represented the location of a trapper's cabin, with the owner's name neatly written beside.

"Watch for moose here," he advised, pointing to a large

circle he had drawn in an open area. Clifford then shared a tale of meeting a bull moose on the trail with his dog team. The moose was unwilling to step off the firm trail into the deep snow. It was all he could do to hold his excited team from running up to the huge creature.

"When moose and dogs tangle, the moose usually wins," he warned. Luckily the moose had eventually stomped off into the bush.

I took another look at the sheet, so I would remember where the moose meadows were. Now each of our maps told a story. One circle in a plain of white warned of a muskeg that might be unfrozen under the snow. Another indicated the location of an impassable tangle of willow. And an *X* marked a creek with open water where we might find otters. With Clifford's pencilled routes and seven eager dogs waiting in the dog yard, we were ready to go.

Namew
Lake

N

Cumberland
Lake

Cumberland
House

Belanger
Lake

Barrier
Lake

Birch
Lake

Watchi
Lake

Saskatchewan River

Saskeram
Lake

Carrot River

The
Pas

- - - - - - -
dogsled route

10 MILES

The Winter Express

Two centuries ago, the North West Company's winter express had relayed packets across the north, raising the spirits of those who were isolated in the remote posts. Swaggering Northmen told tales of thin ice, hungry wolves, and extremes of distance and temperature. Their skill with a dog team was as good a topic for exaggeration as their exploits by paddle and canoe.

With thoughts of tales we would have to tell, Sally and I packed the toboggan just after sunrise on February 8. We were eager to be on the trail again—for the next six weeks, we would sleep in our canvas tent, dine by crackling campfires, and explore the North Country.

The load was heavier than on our previous trip and several inches of new snow slowed the dogs. To keep the team from getting bogged down in snowdrifts, Sally and I alternated between walking and pushing the toboggan.

By the time we stopped for the night in a sheltering grove of spruce, we were exhausted.

"That was a hard-earned sixteen miles," I said, marking our campsite on the map later that evening. With our first resupply stop at The Pas, eighty miles east, we would have to average this distance each day. We had only two extra days of supplies on the toboggan to allow for blizzards or other difficulties.

All night long, snow sifted steadily down. By morning, the tent sagged under the weight of more than six inches of fresh snow. Every shape in the forest was rounded. In exposed places, the snow had blown into deep drifts across the trail.

The new snow made travel even more difficult. Sting pushed through each snowdrift with his chest, breaking trail for the others who followed with less effort. Each time, the other dogs bunched up behind him while he floundered in the powder.

At one particularly high drift, the dogs had just gained their footing as the toboggan rode up onto the drift. Suddenly, the toboggan tipped sideways and slid off the trail. It came to an abrupt stop in a deep hollow.

"We're planted!" I groaned, using the term the voyageurs had coined when a dog team could not keep up with the others.

"Didn't Alexander Henry write that a good voyageur will push till he is nearly knocked out, rather than be planted, even though his load is extra heavy?" Sally said.

"Mmmph." Almost waist-deep in snow, I strained against the back of the toboggan.

"He said it was a matter of pride," Sally prodded as she pulled on the snub rope.

"*Marchez! Marchez!*" I called, urging the team forward. Their willingness to work so hard in difficult conditions inspired me as I watched them strain against the tug-lines. The dogs pulled with every ounce of their strength, heads down, noses almost touching the snow. Finally, the toboggan was back on the trail.

Even with the dogs' Herculean efforts, progress was slow. Our hopes of travelling sixteen miles a day were sinking in the deep snow.

"I think we'd better break trail with the snowshoes," I suggested.

Breaking trail

Clearing trail

Planted!

"You mean *me*," Sally countered. Earlier, we had decided that because the team obeyed a male voice best, I should stay with the dogs to control them. Sally would have to do all the trail breaking.

Sally snowshoed ahead of the dogs for much of the way that day while I pushed the toboggan. Sting eagerly kept up with Sally, sometimes following directly on the heels of her snowshoes.

"Come on, boys!" Sally encouraged as the dogs valiantly struggled through another snowdrift. Sally petted and fussed over each dog, then continued snowshoeing.

Voyageurs had also talked to their dogs, and would curse them roundly if they were slow. Derogatory names included "black frog," "little pig," or even "dead dog." If the dogs were pulling well or running faster than another team, the names might include "good man" or "flyer." The highest praise of all was "that's a DOG!" The Northmen sometimes even encouraged their dogs by singing. For some reason "Alouette" was a favourite.

The wind-packed surface of Belanger Lake offered a brief reprieve for the dogs, but not for Sally. I heard no singing as she snowshoed a trail for the team to follow. Twenty paces after starting out, she pushed her hood back. A short time later she removed her blanket coat and dropped it beside the trail for me to pick up. Despite the cold temperature, she removed her toque, then her wool vest. The dogs didn't need a trail to guide them—they just followed the dotted line of clothing!

For me, holding the team back and always waiting, it seemed to take Sally forever to cross the lake. She plodded along, pausing now and then to catch her breath or adjust her snowshoe bindings.

"Can't you go any faster?" I called to Sally when we caught up with her again. "The voyageurs *ran* from post to post!"

"Hey, we could change jobs," she said, puffing loudly.

"Just teasing," I added quickly, then changed the topic by suggesting lunch.

Sally perched on the edge of the overturned toboggan while I dug out lunch. We munched on slabs of pemmican-like salami and frozen *galette* with cheese. A chunk of chocolate and flask of hot tea completed our simple lunch. Although it wasn't gourmet fare, the high-fat meal refuelled us for the strenuous work and cold weather.

Once off the wind-blown lake, our progress slowed again in the soft snow. The trail led through a tangled area of birch shrub where Clifford had told us to watch for moose. We spied a few meandering tracks, but the creatures who made them were nowhere to be seen.

By three o'clock we had to stop to leave enough daylight for camp chores. However, we had moved forward only ten miles.

"At this pace, it's going to take a long time to reach The Pas," I said as we unhooked the dogs. We were both feeling tired and discouraged. But when I straddled Buck to pull the harness over his head, he reached up and gave me a sloppy, wet lick across my face. I looked over to Sally and saw her rubbing Tom behind the ears.

"What a team!" Sally said, a tired smile on her face. I turned to Buck again and spent a few minutes playing with him in the snow. The miles no longer seemed that important.

A wind overnight packed the snow slightly, and our progress improved the next day. Even so, Sally still had to break trail through the open areas and across each lake. We stopped early to rest Sally's legs, which had become strained from lifting the snowshoes over and over again through the deep snow.

"Here's a quote you might enjoy," I said as we settled into the tent. By candlelight, I read Alexander Henry's words from my journal: "I am now troubled with a disorder, called *mal de raquette*, proceeding from an unusual strain on the tendons of the leg, occasioned by the weight of the snow-shoe. The remedy, prescribed in the country, is that of laying a piece of lighted torchwood on the part, and leaving it there till the flesh is burnt to the nerve; but this experiment, though I had frequently seen it attended with success in others, I did not think proper to make upon myself."

Sally laughed for the first time that day. "I'm cured, I'm cured!" she said. Somehow, learning that others had experienced similar difficulties made her aches more bearable. And realizing that Alexander Henry had suffered the same hardships made us feel closer to him in spirit. As on our canoe journey, we could almost feel his presence each time we read his journal.

That evening, there was plenty to take our minds off our troubles. I repaired Buck's harness where it had torn as a result of his overenthusiastic lunging, and then I replaced a section of tug-line that had been chewed by Blue. Meanwhile, Sally darned a wool mitt that had caught on a tree. Repairs were part of trail life . . . even the tough voyageurs had wielded needles and thread when harnesses needed mending.

The continuing wind made the snow firmer by morning. Sally no longer had to break trail through the open areas, although she still had to lead when we reached untracked snow on Barrier Lake. Once across the lake, the dogs slowed only slightly along the winding trail that led through tangled willows to the Saskatchewan River.

The old trading route now led across the river. As we crossed, we saw why travellers had avoided this river when they could. The ice was rough and jumbled and looked as though the wild waves of the river had frozen instantly in place. Several times, the toboggan tipped precariously as we made our way across the uneven slabs of ice.

Referring to the pencil lines Clifford had drawn on our map, we continued across open meadows, creeks, and small lakes. Slowly but steadily, we inched across the map.

During their winter travels, the voyageurs had stopped every five miles or so to rest the dogs and smoke their pipes. They spoke of a day's journey as being so many *pipes* long, the same term they'd used for their breaks when canoeing in the summer. On well-travelled winter trails, the regular resting-places often had a lean-to and a stack of firewood.

Sally and I measured frozen lakes not in *pipes,* but in "heaves." Heaves represented the number of times I had to wrestle the toboggan onto its side to give Sally time to snowshoe ahead. Birch Lake involved four heaves—about an hour.

As Sally crossed the lake, she kept one eye on a lone tree in the distance so she could snowshoe in a straight line. She also looked back periodically, mentally noting a certain cluster of trees as a marker for our return trip.

The trail led to a narrow part of Saskeram Lake, so this crossing took only two heaves. When we reached the far shore, we were confronted with a wall of marsh grass that towered over our heads. There was no sign of a trail.

"North or south?" Sally asked. I tried to think like the travellers before us. Which route would they have taken? Surely they would have avoided the hill to the north.

"Let's head south along the shore," I suggested. My hunch paid off. We found a tell-tale break in the marsh grass where a creek flowed into the lake. As in the summer, the waterways had been the voyageurs' highway. Wind-blown snow on lakes and smaller rivers made travelling easier than in the forest, although trails led overland between lakes and where the river ice was too jumbled. I found it intriguing that the voyageurs had still called these trails portages, even during winter.

We stopped to make camp where the marsh gave way to willow. Once the team was staked out, Sally collected bunches of tall grass to serve as bedding for the dogs. Each dog eagerly shoved his nose into this straw-substitute and rearranged it until he was comfortable. Blue was almost delirious, pouncing and rolling in the grass. This was much better than the usual spruce boughs. Even Hank settled contentedly on the bed we had prepared for him.

From our camp in the willows, the trail wound through a forest of poplar and spruce, with the usual wild ride as the toboggan careened around each corner. There seemed to be a direct correlation between the speed of the dogs and the twists and turns in the trail—although our shouts and groans as we ducked branches and fought to keep the toboggan on the trail might have had something to do with spurring them on.

We made great progress until the forest thinned and we came to an area where trees had been felled by wind and heavy snow. As we rounded a hairpin corner, a large poplar lay across the trail, blocking our passage.

"Whoa, whoa," I called, throwing the snow hook in. The dogs were eager to go, but the tree lay exactly two feet above the snow—high enough for the dogs to crawl under, but too low to take the toboggan under.

"I'll start," I said, hauling our axe from the *carriole* bag. Fortunately, the dogs didn't seem to mind the commotion of me hacking at the tree. Soon I was overheating, even in the twenty-below morning air. It was hard work with the small hand-wrought axe we had brought. A hundred chops later, I cut through one side. Another hundred and the tree fell into the snow with a muffled plop.

Only ten minutes later, it was Sally's turn to chop through the next tree.

"Something tells me this trail hasn't been used for a while," I said when we stopped just around the next corner to clear another fallen tree. Finally, the trees gave way to open lowlands of willow again.

By mid-afternoon of our fifth day we were nearing The Pas, where we planned to stay a night with John and Shirley Calvert, the mushers who had generously loaned us Sting. The trail split and I was just about to pull out the map when Sting's ears perked forward and he veered to the left. He increased the team's speed to a fast trot and led us towards the Carrot River.

Sting seemed to know where he was going, so I let him choose our route. Without hesitation, he guided the team across the river then up the other bank, directly to John Calvert's dog yard. Twenty dogs began howling as we pulled up. What a welcome!

"I knew Sting would get you here," John said, eyes crinkling as he came to greet us. I could sense him silently

Taking a well-earned rest

Showing Sting the map

207

assessing our team, the harnesses, and the toboggan load.

After patting Sting, John walked to the back of the toboggan and gripped the handlebars.

"This brings back a lot of memories," he said, flexing his knees over imaginary bumps. I had an idea we would spend the evening hearing all about them.

In our capacity as mail runners we handed him a package from a friend at Cumberland House, telling him about a race planned for the third week of March. Although John was in his late seventies, he still had a passion for dogsled racing.

"This might be my last season," John confessed as he showed us dozens of trophies from races spanning three decades.

"He says that every year," Shirley added with a chuckle.

Over supper, John told us about his days of travel by dog team and toboggan when he had worked his trap line.

"My dogs were smart. Without me even asking, they always stopped at each trap. The only problem was, even if I had removed a trap weeks earlier the dogs still stopped. I had to walk to where the traps had been and pretend to check them before the dogs would leave!"

John went on to tell us tales of other experiences he'd had when travelling with his dogs. He launched into a story about a savage wolf, complete with flaming eyes and flashing fangs, chasing him down a trail until he hit it over the head with his tea kettle.

"Hmmm, that wolf sounds closely related to a grizzly Ian once met up with," Sally said, smiling.

Our conversation turned to tales of nights on the trail.

"Didn't use a tent," John said. "I just made a lean-to from spruce branches. If it was really cold I'd bring in two or three dogs. I'd have the fire on one side of me and the dogs on the other."

Sally seemed to like that idea, but I wasn't so sure about sharing a blanket with a couple of dogs. Everything we wore, from mitts to moccasins, already smelled of dog.

While Shirley kept us fuelled with tea and cookies, John

continued talking. He was enjoying sharing his stories with a new audience, and his blue eyes sparkled as he reminisced. Sally and I hung on every word, embellished or not.

We stayed with John and Shirley for two nights to let the dogs rest and to fill their stomachs with fresh meat. Meanwhile, Sally and I took the opportunity to fill our stomachs with Shirley's home-cooked meals. Like voyageurs of the past, this stop was an occasion to enjoy good company and to take a break from trail food and hard work.

On February 14 we continued our journey, loaded down with ten days of supplies. The old trail crossed the Saskatchewan River again then turned north-east. Gradually, the scenery changed from lowland to rolling hills of pine and aspen. The hilly terrain was a pleasant change from the flat, marshy country that we had passed through so far. We continued across the undulating landscape, dropping to Watchi Lake, climbing a wooded slope, and then descending to a chain of small lakes in the next valley.

On our second day, patches of blue had broken through the grey-flannel sky. For the first time in more than a week, we saw the sun. It radiated little warmth this time of year and a cold north wind chilled us as the clearing sky brought lower temperatures. By late afternoon, a blanket of cold air had settled over the valley.

That night we gathered extra spruce boughs for the dogs and shovelled snow around the tent for insulation. Sally and I huddled close to the fire, warming our bodies before crawling into cold blankets that had been on the toboggan all day.

"Can't get much colder," we repeated each time we woke and added more clothing in an effort to keep warm. By morning the thin red line in our thermometer indicated minus thirty-five degrees.

Our first priority was a campfire and hot tea. Although the dogs could eat snow through the day, we had to drink mug after mug of tea to make up for moisture lost in the cold, dry air. We had become used to the distinctive snowmelt flavour and the garnish of spruce needles floating in our mugs.

The dogs were used to the sounds of clanging pots now, and even slept through the din of Sally beating frost from the canvas tent. Only one or two raised their heads as we packed up camp and loaded the toboggan. However, when we approached with harnesses in hand, they all came alive. They jumped up from their beds, howling and lunging in anticipation of another day on the trail.

An hour after we set out, the wind picked up, bringing the windchill factor to minus forty-five. Each dog's breath rose into the frigid air, wreathing their fur in hoar-frost. Their saliva froze into icy beards, and looked especially comical on the black fur of Link, Tom, and Blue.

"You look just like the dogs," Sally said, laughing. My eyebrows and beard, as well as my toque and the hood of my blanket coat had become coated with white rime.

My exposed face was taut and numb. Even my hands and feet were cold, despite heavy mitts and many layers of socks. I could tell Sally's toes were cold by the way she knocked her moccasins together, trying to encourage circulation.

When the dogs slowed to their all-day trot, Sally jumped off the toboggan and began to run. Hank and Buck, at the rear of the team, looked over their shoulders now and then to see what she was up to. Once Sally had warmed up I took my turn. Jogging behind the toboggan eventually pounded warmth back into my numb feet.

The voyageurs had called this *courir et rouler*, the expression for alternately running and riding on the toboggan. This method worked well enough, except that running in soft snow was exhausting, and the cold air seared our lungs with each deep breath.

Back on the toboggan, I removed a mitt and held my bare hand against my face, warming one cheek then the other. I felt a lump on my left cheek—the first sign of frostbite. After my face had thawed, I put my hands inside my blanket coat, tucking them under my armpits.

A Northman would never have complained of cold or frostbite. In fact, one traveller had written: "Anyone who expects much sympathy for such trifling misery in this country, will be left to wipe his own eyes. If one gets frozen or starved, he may expect ridicule, not condolence. The old voyageurs will take great pains to cache a frost bite, or any fatigue."

Sally and I didn't see any point in complaining either. Being cold much of the day, especially at this temperature, was just part of winter travel. I willed myself to be warm, to ignore my cold face, fingers, and numbed toes. When my ice-covered eyelashes stuck together and my nose lost all sensation, I suggested a lunch stop.

I halted the dogs at a natural wind-break of trees. While Sally dug out a snack from the grub box, I collected dry twigs and branches for a campfire. In the reverse of a summer fire, I started with large sticks to create an insulating bed to prevent the fire from sinking into the snow. Then I placed tinder and small sticks on top and lit the fire.

"Ten minutes . . . not bad," Sally said as she reached out to warm her fingers over the flames.

"And that included gathering the firewood," I boasted. My self-praise was interrupted when Sally pointed out that the pot was still full of unmelted snow.

I moved closer to the fire and felt the heat melting the ice from my beard. Later, when I sipped a mug of tea, I felt warm for the first time since we'd left camp. However, the warmth was fleeting. The mug that had warmed my hands quickly cooled, and by the time I'd drained the tea, ice crystals had formed around the rim.

While Sally and I warmed ourselves by the fire, the dogs took the opportunity to groom themselves and look after their paws. Several of the dogs chewed out lumps of snow that had wedged between their pads.

"Poor Link . . . he's bleeding," Sally said, noticing several dots of red in the snow.

"So is Hank," I said after I had checked the other dogs. At

this cold temperature, the snow had become granular. To protect the dogs' paws from the coarse snow, we decided to put booties on their feet. Years ago, booties were made from deerskin, but hungry dogs often chewed them off their feet. Our less-edible booties were made from thick fabric and were shaped like small socks.

Putting booties on a hyperactive dog was quite a procedure. In fact, it made our first attempts at harnessing the dogs seem easy in comparison.

"Hold still!" Sally groaned as she wrestled with Blue. It was almost impossible to single-handedly hold a wriggling, uncooperative creature and slip a bootie onto a flailing paw.

"I'll hold him, you put the boots on," I suggested after her fourth attempt. I pinned him down and whispered soothing words into an ear.

"You never whisper in my ear like that," Sally teased.

"I would if I had to put your socks on while kneeling in the snow!"

Working together, we managed to force a bootie onto each foot. Twenty-eight paws later, all the dogs were ready to go.

The dogs weren't sure what to think of the booties tied to their feet. Hank stared at his paws, head tilted and a quizzical look on his face. Blue had already pulled his front booties off and Tom was about to. We re-booted Blue, then quickly continued on our way.

For the first few minutes the dogs pranced down the trail, lifting each paw unusually high as they became accustomed to the strange objects on their feet. Even so, in three hours of travel, we lost only two booties—one in deep snow and another during the excitement of a pile-up.

At the end of the day, Sally and I patted the dogs and checked them over, looking for rub marks from the harnesses and for other problems. It was like having seven children to care for as we inspected their fur and their feet. When Tom developed a cough, we worried. Was he sick? I listened carefully to his breathing, not really sure what I was trying to detect. When Hank developed a raw patch on his rump where a tug-line rubbed, we applied ointments from our first-aid kit.

Our ritual of petting and ear rubbing was a wonderful way to end each day, for us as well as the dogs. The dogs loved the attention. They nuzzled against us, and even rolled onto their backs for us to scratch their stomachs. In fact, each dog seemed jealous of the time we spent with the dog beside him. When I tried to move down the line to visit Jeff, Link blocked my passage with a nudge of his shoulder. Meanwhile, Jeff sat with pleading eyes, whining softly as he waited for his turn.

Sally lingered with Tom, warming her fingers in his fur. "Maybe we could bring Tom into the tent tonight to keep us warm," she hinted.

Did I feel a tinge of jealousy, too? "There isn't enough room . . . and besides, he snores," I countered.

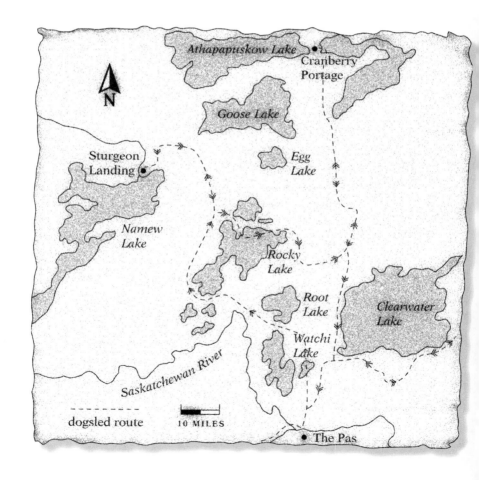

Athapapuskow Lake
Cranberry Portage
Goose Lake
Egg Lake
Sturgeon Landing
Namew Lake
Rocky Lake
Root Lake
Clearwater Lake
Watchi Lake
Saskatchewan River
The Pas

- - - - dogsled route   10 MILES

N

SEVENTEEN

Exploring

Seven mounds of fur lay curled up in the snow, noses under tails as Sally and I crawled out of the tent. The morning was clear and cold, and a thick layer of hoarfrost coated each bush, each twig, and each dog.

"Hey, Sting," I called. My breath swirled around my shoulders like a white scarf. As Sting lifted his head to greet me, frost crystals flew from his fur, tinkling audibly when they landed in the snow. With a wide canine yawn, he stood up and stretched, becoming engulfed in the fog from his warm breath.

"Morning, boys," I called to the others while I stroked Sting's thick fur. Several tails wagged in response to my voice. As I greeted each dog, warming my fingers in their fur, I could think of no better way to start a day.

"Frozen blankets, anyone?" Sally called from the tent. She had started packing up camp and was holding a frosty blanket by a corner. It hung stiffly, like a sheet of birchbark.

"No wonder we felt cold last night," I said as I helped her shake out the frost then fold the stiffened wool. It took our combined effort to wrestle the rigid canvas tent to the ground and roll it into a bundle. We paused several times to warm our hands by the fire.

When the dogs saw us pack the toboggan then pull out the harnesses, they began their usual howling and barking. Hook-up, though, was not as wild as it had been on our first days. They had learned we weren't going anywhere until the stake-out chain had been stowed on the toboggan. Like racers at a starting line, they leaned forward, ready for the signal to go.

The dogs seemed energized by the cold weather and ran at a brisk trot all morning. At lunch time, we stopped near the settlement of Sturgeon Landing on the shore of Namew Lake. During the fur trade there had been a small outpost here, one of almost eighty scattered across the country. As dog-drivers of the winter express, bearing news and parcels from other posts, we would have been given a warm welcome and tot of rum when we arrived.

Now, with only a scattering of houses along the lakeshore, the only greeting we received was from several dogs who were running loose. I suppose if voyageurs had seen these strays, they might have hitched them to their toboggan.

"Marchez!" I called to our team, urging them on. There was no need to stop—we already had a full complement of fine sled dogs.

Three hours later, the dogs began to tire. We had easily achieved our daily goal, and when the trail wound through a spruce forest, Sally suggested that we stop early and build a lean-to as the Northmen had during their travels.

"It'll be romantic," she added. "You and me curled up by the fire . . . "

I suspected that a smoking fire and prickly bed of spruce boughs might dampen the spirit of romance somewhat, but agreed anyway. Surely, it couldn't be any colder than sleeping in a frosty tent.

Once the dogs were bedded down, we began building our shelter. We lashed a pole between two standing trees and leaned other poles against this crossbar to form a sloping roof. Then I thatched the roof with spruce boughs that Sally had gathered from nearby trees.

"Looks good . . . but it took four times as long as setting up the tent," I commented when we finally completed the roof. Even so, I could see that voyageurs would have found it useful to have a number of these shelters along a well-used trading route.

I built a campfire one pace from the front of the lean-to, with a wall of logs to reflect the heat towards us and to draw away the smoke. Looking forward to a cozy evening, we settled onto a cushion of spruce boughs.

While supper cooked over the fire, Sally wrote in her journal, holding her pencil in a mittened hand and leaning close to the flames for warmth and light. Meanwhile, I began my nightly ritual of drying mitts, felt liners, and socks over the fire. The scent of wet wool and wood smoke mixed agreeably with the aroma of pea soup simmering over the coals. We always enjoyed this part of the evening when we could relax and reflect on the events of the day.

A shower of sparks illuminated the scene as I added another log to the fire. Red coals were rimmed with white ashes. A wisp of smoke drifted over the lean-to, carried by the night breeze.

"It's magical out here," Sally said, putting her journal aside.

"It is," I agreed, moving closer to her. "In the city we never take the time to look at the stars." We were more at home here sitting in the snow than in the most comfortable chair. Here, there were no walls, no ceilings, no constraints.

Gazing at the night sky, we searched among the brilliant points of light for the North Star, and found it above the cup of the Big Dipper. Closer to the horizon, a faint glow of the aurora borealis shimmered in white curtains. A second band of light came from above and intensified until the lights merged into one bright glow. The aurora rippled along the horizon, then faded until we could see only a stray beam here and there.

In the forest, strange shapes and shadows were cast across the snow. Most were as still as the winter night, although now and then, a shadow moved across the scene.

Tea break on the trail

A cozy evening in a lean-to

Not far away a snowshoe hare, barely visible against a white backdrop, scampered through the forest.

Although Sally and I loved being outdoors more than anywhere else, the lean-to was not as comfortable as we'd hoped it would be. Our backs were cold, still coated with frost, while our fronts were overcooked by the heat of the fire. Once we were under the wool blankets, a breeze wafted through the open lean-to, negating the meagre warmth from the flames. Worst of all, one of us had to crawl out of bed every hour or two and stoke the fire.

"Romantic enough for you?" I asked as we shivered together under the spruce canopy the next morning.

"A charming hideaway," Sally replied, pulling the blanket up to her nose, "but I think I'll stick with the tent, after all."

One advantage of the lean-to was that breaking camp was much faster without pegs to pull or stiff canvas to fold and pack away. We tied our load onto the toboggan, hooked up seven frosty dogs, and started down the trail in record time.

The cold oak boards of the toboggan flexed and creaked more loudly than usual as they undulated over the trail. The sisal rope rigging had shrunk in the cold and was now fiddle-string tight. Thinking of Solomon's warning that we would break our toboggan, we stopped the team. With cold-numbed hands, I struggled to untie then retie the knots of the rigging.

The country had become more hilly, and by early afternoon the dogs trotted past rugged rock outcrops. We were back among the high bluffs and glacier-gouged lakes and valleys of the Canadian Shield.

On the winding descent to Rocky Lake, the dogs ran flat out. Now and then, I dragged my foot to control the speed of the toboggan. For most of the way I just hung on and enjoyed the wild ride. Sally perched on top of the load, with one hand gripping a lashing rope and the other holding the snow hook in case we had to stop in a hurry.

Rocky Lake was aptly named for its rugged shoreline. High outcrops of rock were splashed with orange lichen, adding colour to a landscape of white and green. It was such a stunning scene that we stopped to enjoy the view.

After a few minutes Buck and Link began to bark, impatient to go. The bluffs echoed the sound of their barking until it seemed as if several teams were travelling with us. I imagined a team of Alexander Henry's finest dogs pulling up beside us.

"*Monsieur*, your dogs look slow today," taunted a red-toqued spectre of a Northman.

"They are faster than wolves," I retorted, under my breath.

"Old wolves perhaps . . . "

That insult could only be countered by the challenge to race.

Sally gave me a strange look when I ran to the toboggan.

"Ready?" I called, picking up the hook. Surprised by my unusual haste, Sally dropped the *galette* she had been nibbling and gripped the ropes.

I shouted the command to go. Seven startled dogs leaped forward as I urged them on. Snow flew from their paws. Wind whistled past my ears. My shouts of encouragement were repeated by the bluff. Or was it my opponent?

"They're gaining on us!" I called to Sally.

"Who? What?"

I jumped off the toboggan and ran, legs pumping, feet punching into the soft snow. Like a demented voyageur I shouted hoarsely to my team. The dogs sensed the urgency in my voice and picked up the pace.

The shadow of a tall tree marked the finish line. I looked behind me. There was no competitor to be seen.

"We lost them!" I cackled, stopping the team just as we crossed the finish line. Seven dogs panted happily. Sally looked at me, then the dogs, then back again.

She listened quietly as I explained what the echoing bluffs had conjured up in my mind.

"I think you've been reading too much from Henry's journal," she concluded, shaking her head.

If Sally and I had been accompanied by other teams, custom would have decreed that each team take a "spell ahead" to break trail. Instead, we had to push our toboggan up the steep hill from the lake through untracked snow.

Fortunately, the dogs were strong from several weeks of arduous work. For the next two hours, the trail rose and fell as we traversed a series of hills, each higher than the one before. Although it was far below freezing, we rested the dogs frequently so they wouldn't overheat. The long climb ended at a ridge high above the valley.

From a bluff we had our first panoramic view since arriving in this part of the country last fall. Below us, Rocky Lake sat in a ring of dark evergreens. Beyond that, unnamed bumps and lakes dotted the land. In the distance the Saskatchewan River meandered through the scene, a blue-grey shadow curving back and forth across the white land. Farther south the low, rounded form of the Pasquia Hills was the only landmark on a flat plain that stretched as far as the eye could see.

For two days, we alternated between struggling up steep hills and hurtling down others as the trail continued north towards Cranberry Portage. On the downhill runs, the dogs stretched out, enjoying the speed as much as we did. Several times, Sally had to drag her snow hook to slow the toboggan as we careened around hairpin turns.

One switchback was so abrupt that Sally had to leap off, snub rope in hand, and heave sideways to help me steer the toboggan. Her moccasins skidded on the snow, a spray of white showering from her feet as she slid down the slope. At the back, I leaned far to one side to counteract the tipping load as the toboggan slewed around the corner.

"Jump on!" I called and Sally flung herself onto the speeding toboggan.

"The flatlands will seem pretty dull after this!" Sally said when we reached the bottom. Seven dogs wagged their tails, as if to agree with her statement.

In this hilly terrain, the dogs were expending a lot more energy than they had earlier. Although we wanted to feed them more to compensate for the extra work, we had only enough food at normal rations to reach our next pickup point. The dogs began to sniff at things by the side of the trail—a hole in the snow, droppings left by wolves, and the remains of a hare killed by an owl. When Buck tried to gnaw at the babiche on Sally's snowshoes, we realized the dogs were very hungry. At feeding time each evening, they became more frenzied than ever.

I had to admit that I was feeling hungry as well. Over the past week, Sally and I had sewed pleats in the waistbands of our trousers as we lost weight. At the beginning of the trip, a daily ration of almost twice the calories we had consumed during our days of training had been sufficient for us and the dogs. Now we devoured every meal and scraped every last morsel from the pots. I might have been tempted to eat some of the dogs' rations as well, if they had been eating whitefish or low-grade pemmican as teams had during voyageur days.

When we reached the settlement of Cranberry Portage on February 24, I raided the first store we had seen since The Pas. Going for calories, I stocked up on chocolate bars and bags of peanuts for Sally and me, as well as several boxes of lard for the dogs. These would augment the supplies waiting for us at this resupply post.

"Did you get lots of chocolate?" Sally asked when I returned.

"More than Henry had," I replied.

We chuckled each time we read his words: "The last remains of our provisions were expended, but I had taken the precaution to conceal a cake of chocolate in the carriole . . . The kettle being filled with water, I put into it one square of the chocolate. The quantity was scarcely sufficient to alter the colour of the water; but, each of us drank half a gallon of the warm liquor, by which we were much refreshed. In the morning, we allowed ourselves a similar repast, after finishing which, we marched vigorously for six hours."

With our toboggan-load of new supplies, including chocolate, Sally and I explored the country around Cranberry Portage. Then we retraced our route over the ridge trail, and continued south along the shoreline of Clearwater Lake.

A few days later, the temperature warmed to minus ten

degrees and travelling became more pleasant. We removed one layer of bulky clothing and were able to work with gloves instead of cumbersome mitts. With the warmer weather, chickadees and snow buntings became more active, often accompanying us with their cheerful calls. At our lunch stops, gray jays glided down on outstretched wings, whistling softly.

Days blended together with the rhythm of life on the trail, from harnessing the dogs each morning to setting up camp each evening. I think the dogs enjoyed travelling, seeing new country, and wondering what was around the next bend—a deer, a long downhill grade, or a run into the wind across an open meadow.

After more than three weeks of travel, our trail companions had become accustomed to our daily routines. When we stopped and turned the toboggan on its side, they knew the break would be more than a few minutes. Sometimes they used the opportunity to eat snow and quench their thirst or to chew ice from between their toes. And when the dogs saw us pull out our lunch, they lay down for a snooze. All except Tom. We had never once seen him sit or lie down, except at the end of the day.

At one lunch stop, Sally tried to convince Tom to take a break. She knelt beside him and stroked his fur.

"Sit, Tom," she said, pushing down on his rump. He stood at attention, leaning forward into his harness. She repeated her command and pushed down even harder. I was about to suggest that you can't teach an old dog new tricks when he finally sat down.

"Good boy!" she praised. To my surprise, he remained sitting as Sally walked back to the toboggan. Even so, he was the first one to stand at attention when we flipped the toboggan upright.

"You know, Tom is the smallest but the hardest worker," Sally said.

"He reminds me of you," I laughed, tugging on her toque.

As we sped across the snow that afternoon, I was mesmerized by the alternating bands of sunlight and shadows of trees across the trail. Long-legged silhouettes of the dogs wove in and out of the forest beside us, appearing then disappearing in the shadows.

Sally and I were lulled into a sense of well-being as we rode on the toboggan. With hardly a command, the dogs trotted down the trail. Now and then, a dog would scoop up a mouthful of snow without breaking stride. At each bend in the trail Hank leaned into the left or right tug-line, guiding the toboggan around the corner.

Usually the dogs ran with tails hanging loosely and ears relaxed, except when they heard a bird or animal in the forest. Then all ears perked forward. Occasionally, a ptarmigan flushed up and glided down the trail ahead of us. Each time, the dogs increased their speed to give chase, ignoring the weight of the toboggan behind them.

Sally and I thought this was great sport until the dogs darted into the forest after a cackling bird. Caught off guard, we weren't prepared for the branches that whipped across our faces, or for the spray of snow that blinded us. With a splintering crash, the toboggan came to an abrupt halt against a tree. Sally kept on going and tumbled into the snow—head first.

Now, hopelessly tangled in the tug-lines, the dogs stood quietly and waited for us to sort out the mess. On our first outings, a similar experience would have set them fighting.

"Having a grand adventure?" I said, ruffling Sting's fur as I untangled his lines. Part of the change in the dogs was a reflection of the change in us. During our first runs, we probably would have been shouting anxiously at our dogs as we rushed forward to separate them.

I looked over to Sally as she gently unwrapped a line from Link's front leg.

"I think he's hurt," Sally reported, working her fingers down his leg. Link whined softly as I walked over to check him.

"His leg seems okay," Sally said, "but he won't put weight on it."

Stopping here for the night was out of the question, as

there was no place to pitch our tent or tie out the dogs. After a brief discussion, Sally and I decided to continue along the trial, but to stop as soon as we could.

Link limped slightly during the short run to Clearwater Lake, but did not complain. We pitched our tent at a scenic campsite and decided to take the next day off. Since leaving The Pas, we had travelled nearly three hundred miles, and all of us were tired.

"I'd say a day of rest and double rations would be just what the vet would order," I said, adding several extra scoops of dog food into the pots.

Sally and I lounged in the tent until late the following morning, lazily watching shadows creep down the frosted walls. Because the tent remained standing, the dogs seemed to realize this was a day off. They slept all day, occasionally rising to stretch or water a shrub, then keeling over on their beds of marsh grass to snooze again.

By afternoon the temperature had warmed enough for Sally and me to lounge in the sun without our heavy blanket coats.

"I'd say a bath is in order!" Sally announced as she built up a roaring fire.

"You, me, or the dogs?" I asked. Sally's pointing finger left no doubt that I was the intended subject.

While seven dogs looked on, I removed layer after layer of clothing, then stood on spruce boughs by the warmth of the fire. After weeks of hurried sponge baths, the stream of warm water that Sally poured over my body felt luxurious. Ah, bliss! Then the pot ran dry.

"More water!" I pleaded as goose-bumps turned to shivers.

"Nope. You've had your share," Sally replied, handing me a towel the size of a dishcloth. I dried off, then threw on several layers of clothing rather frantically.

"Shall I ask the dogs to look the other way?" I inquired as Sally took her turn. It would have been in vain—Sally's shrieks when she stumbled barefoot from the spruce-bough mat into knee-deep snow caused every dog to watch our antics. If they thought we were crazy, however, they didn't show it.

Refreshed and well rested, we travelled twenty-five miles the next day. Link no longer limped and the dogs were eager to run. Following a trail around Clearwater Lake, we travelled through sun-drenched birch forests and narrow passages shaded with canopies of low, overhanging spruce.

For the first time since starting our winter journey, Sally and I removed our toques as the temperature soared to just below freezing. We enjoyed the simple, almost forgotten pleasure of the wind ruffling our hair. For three days we explored around the south-east end of the lake. When our food supply ran low, we turned the toboggan back towards The Pas.

Another three days and one ptarmigan chase later, we pulled into John Calvert's yard. Now we had our own tales of the trail to share. We spent the evening telling him of the cold weather, our night in the lean-to, wild downhill runs, and other events of our journey.

The next morning, John looked on wistfully as we harnessed the dogs for our return trip to Cumberland House. At one point, as I wrestled with Buck, I glanced up at John. Our eyes met and I understood the yearning for adventure I saw there. If John had still owned a toboggan, I'm sure he would have hitched up a team and come with us.

"Have a safe journey, mushers," he said. Sally and I nodded, then I released the snub rope. With that, our dogs sprinted down the slope to the Carrot River.

EIGHTEEN

A Northern Spring

As we crossed Saskeram Lake, Sally rode with me on the toboggan, her trail-worn snowshoes tucked under the tarp. Even though our previous tracks had been scoured by wind and covered by new snow, Sting confidently led the team across the open expanse. Once or twice, I gently called "Gee" or "Haw" to guide him to the landmarks on the far side. How different this was from five weeks earlier!

Now we flew over the snow, seven strong dogs pulling us across Saskeram and Birch Lakes in one day. All went well until we came to the Saskatchewan River, which was covered in a layer of slush. The change in temperature had caused the ice to crack, and water had flooded over top, saturating the snow. All we could do was camp and hope the water would freeze overnight.

By morning the river had become a sheet of ice. Nervously, I thumped the ice ahead of me with a pole, testing its thickness before we hooked up the team. I'd read that if the ice didn't crack under a thumped pole, it would hold a person. Hoping the book was reliable, I tapped my way along. Sally cheerfully called after me that the long pole would bridge a hole if I fell through.

"The ice seems solid," I reported, shuffling my way back across the river. I reasoned that, although the toboggan was much heavier than I was, its weight would be distributed over a larger area and would not crack the ice.

"Sounds like a good theory—but I vote for a high-speed crossing!" Sally added.

With some trepidation, we hooked up the team. The dogs started with their usual abandon, but as we neared the ice, the tug-lines went slack. Just as Sting reached the edge, the others stopped in their tracks. Several of the dogs stood with legs locked and bodies trembling, holding Sting back.

"So much for speed," said Sally.

"Why don't you go ahead . . . maybe they'll follow you," I suggested.

Sally stepped tentatively onto the ice, barely managing to stay on her feet.

"Come on, boys, you can do it," she called. As each dog stepped onto the ice, legs splayed out and toenails clattered on the slippery surface. Even so, they followed Sally, slipping and sliding across the ice. The dogs had come to trust us completely.

I held my breath, my heart beating loudly as the ice creaked and groaned under the toboggan. Slowly, cautiously, the dogs followed Sally. When the toboggan finally slid onto firm snow at the other side, I urged the team to run faster. Seven dogs broke into a run for momentum up the steep bank.

"I think they've earned their pompoms," I said after we had crested the hill. Voyageurs had dressed up their teams in blankets, bells, and baubles when they approached the forts, to show their pride in their dogs. We stopped our team for a rest and dug out the wool balls that were buried in a pack.

"And to Sting, the red-and-green pompom award for bravery in crossing icy rivers," Sally said with mock solemnity as she tied it onto his harness.

I'm not sure, but it seemed to me that each dog stood a

bit taller as we attached a pompom and several bells to his harness. With pompoms bouncing from side to side and bells jangling, the dogs headed down the trail as proudly as any team might have two centuries before.

"If that phantom voyageur challenges us now, we're ready," Sally said.

I nodded in agreement, and laughed. "No one would dare challenge a team as well dressed as ours!" I replied.

By noon the next day, the snow had turned to the consistency of the porridge we had eaten for breakfast. The temperature had risen to above freezing—a warmth we hadn't experienced for more than six months. When we stopped to give the team a rest, seven panting dogs sprawled on the snow to cool off.

We were able to continue for only another hour before the dogs began to punch deep holes in the soft snow. The dogs also had to work extra hard to pull the water-soaked toboggan that dragged reluctantly across the snow. There was no point in working the team to exhaustion. We made camp.

Sally and I rose long before sunrise and packed up the tent by the light of our candle-lantern. Our plan was to get an early start and travel as far as possible while the snow was relatively firm. We had read that voyageurs often travelled at night, but I wondered how they knew where they were going. Perhaps they had relied on their dogs to find the way.

"You hold the lantern and I'll harness the dogs," Sally suggested as we finished loading the toboggan.

The dogs were reluctant to rise from their spruce-bough beds when we wakened them well ahead of their usual hour, but they sleepily complied as Sally harnessed them in the semi-darkness. Once the dogs were hooked to the toboggan they were as eager as ever to run. From the back, I could see only the vague silhouettes of seven leaping figures in the pre-dawn light.

"Ready?" I felt the dogs take up the slack of the tug-lines.

At the handlebars of the toboggan

A well-dressed team

I released the snub rope and the toboggan jerked ahead, as if propelled by an unseen force. Blurred shapes of trees swept past as the dogs pulled us at a fast trot. Sting led unerringly, following the twists and turns of the trail as easily as if it were daylight. Our eyesight was not as keen as the dogs' though, and we had some trouble seeing where we were going.

"Watch out for the . . . " Sally called just before a dark form snatched the toque from my head.

As I clutched my toque with one hand, I felt the sled veer to the left, and instinctively leaned into the corner. Bells tinkled and dogs panted in the darkness. It was exhilarating, and a bit eerie, to be careening blindly down the trail.

As the first blush of dawn illuminated the forest, chickadees began calling. Then came the chattering of squirrels and drumming of spruce grouse. Slowly, the forest came alive with a medley of birdsong.

Four hours later, the snow had softened from the warmth of the sun. We stopped again and made camp. Sally and I spent the afternoon drying soggy socks and moccasins over a campfire.

"Any ideas how to make the toboggan slide better?" I asked as we sat by the fire. The linseed oil had long ago worn off and the wood was now saturated with water, making it difficult for the dogs to pull. Though we had only a day or so of travel left, the toboggan could not be used as it was.

Sally's idea of coating the toboggan with lard that we carried for the dogs seemed reasonable at first. Then, after thinking it through, I burst into laughter.

"Great idea . . . except the dogs might decide the toboggan smells like supper!" My suggestion of cooking oil met with equal scepticism from Sally.

"How about wax? It works for skis," Sally said, after we had rejected several other ideas. I perked up when I remembered the extra candles that we carried in our emergency kit.

After drying the base of the toboggan by the fire, we rubbed a candle over the warm wood. We improved on our original idea by melting the wax into the wood with the bottom of an empty pot heated over the fire. The result was a slick, polished surface.

The next day, the toboggan slid smoothly across the wet snow. Although we could have travelled all the way to Cumberland House that day, we made camp just a few miles short of our destination. As on our canoe trip, Sally and I yearned for one more night in the tent before ending our journey.

Sally and I lingered at the campfire longer than usual that evening. I pulled out my jaw harp and began to twang a voyageur tune. Buck howled in accompaniment.

A little nostalgic on this last evening, we reminisced about winding forest trails and exhilarating downhill runs.

"I suppose we were lured north by the places we would see, the adventures we would have," Sally said reflectively. "Now I realize that perhaps the real reason was to challenge ourselves, to tackle things we had never done before."

I thought back to the start of our journey—the planning, the letters we wrote, the effort it took to make the trip reality. During our research, we had seen the word "perseverance" on a crest painted on a voyageur canoe. It had been the motto of the North West Company. During the year, it had also become ours.

"It took a lot of perseverance to train our crew of underdogs," I said, thinking back to our first days. "But they became a great team!"

"Mmm," Sally agreed, leaning her head on my shoulder. "We couldn't have asked for better trail companions."

Sting had overcome his initial shyness and was now a confident leader who obeyed every command. Link had grown from an inexperienced freight dog to a competent team member. His unbridled enthusiasm added excitement to every event, from hook-up to chasing ptarmigan.

Jeff, who had been a reluctant leader, had risen to the challenge of guiding the team across wind-blown lakes. Buck had become my favourite, and not just because of his sloppy kisses. He worked consistently, even through the deepest snow. Then came Tom. What he lacked in size, he made up for with heart. He was always eager to pull, always leaning into the harness.

Blue, the scrawny youngster, had grown to a strong, barrel-chested work dog. And finally there was Hank, the instigator of the first fights, who now got along with every other dog. He still had a habit of grabbing mitts and sashes, but we forgave him these minor transgressions.

I thought of what Alexander Henry had said of his dogs: "There is no animal, with which I am acquainted, that would be able to render the service that our dogs do, in this country, where the snow is very deep in the winter season. They ask for little more than a chunk of pemmican each day, and give much in return."

Our dogs had certainly given us a great deal in return for their daily feed. They had pulled us more than six hundred miles, and were as enthusiastic now as they had been at the start of our journey. Through snowstorms and across thin ice, our trail companions had been unquestioningly faithful.

The dogs had inspired us with their tenacity as they pulled with all of their strength through drift after drift of deep snow. They had taught us patience when we had to coax them across glare ice or untangle them from twisted tug-lines. Mostly, the dogs had shown us what teamwork could accomplish.

The next morning, Sally and I packed up camp and hooked our team to the toboggan. Then, for one last day, we experienced the thrill of speeding down the trail as our seven dogs eagerly leaned into their harnesses. For one last day, snow from the dogs' feet flew through the air, landing on Sally's face as she sat at the front of the toboggan. With the back of her mitt, she wiped wet snow from her eyes. Near the end of our journey, I tried to call "Gee" at a fork in the trail, but had trouble speaking. Sting and the team took the correct turn without guidance.

When we arrived at the dog yard, Sally and I took longer than usual unharnessing the dogs, checking them over, and petting them. During the past weeks, living with the dogs day and night, we had come to know their virtues and their foibles. Each one had become a special friend.

Sally fussed over each dog, then buried her face in Tom's fur, talking softly.

"I wish we could take them home with us," she murmured, her eyes moist. We had talked of this many times over the last few days, but each time we had come to the conclusion that the dogs belonged here.

"I couldn't imagine the dogs being happy with any life but the one they have," I replied gently.

"I know, but I'll miss them . . . especially Tom," Sally said. Smiling, I reminded her that she had once been afraid of Tom's bark. Since then he had become Sally's favourite.

As we walked away from the yard, the dogs began to howl. Was it my imagination, or was their howling more mournful than on other occasions? We stopped to listen, and I realized that I knew each voice. Sting led the session, accompanied by the baritone howls of Buck and Hank. Jeff and Blue howled soprano, their voices breaking on the highest notes. Link interjected his staccato barks, and Tom ended the song with his deep, mournful wail.

Sally took my hand, silently pulling me away.

The dogs enjoyed a well-earned rest, while we packed our belongings and looked for a good home for the team. For the time being, the dogs were content to snooze the days away in beds of fresh straw and to stay in one place for a while.

We returned Sting to John Calvert, then asked around Cumberland House to see if any mushers would like the other dogs. To take our minds off the thought of parting with our trail companions, Sally and I retrieved our canoe from the shed where we had stored it. As I tapped the ribs back into place, I thought of the voyageurs of long ago. The ritual of refitting ribs would have been part of their spring as well. This time of year, everyone at the North West Company trading post would have been busy preparing for the annual trip to Grand Portage. In addition to repairing canoes, men would have been packing pemmican into canvas sacks and bundling furs into ninety-pound bales.

I imagined the men pausing in their work to watch geese, as we did, with anticipation. The arrival of migratory birds meant the waterways were gradually opening. Before long, the voyageurs would have exchanged toboggans and dogs for canoes and paddles.

I wondered if the voyageurs had become as attached to their dogs as we had. In a way, Clifford Carrière answered that question when he came to visit us at the dog yard.

"I've often wished I could travel with dogs again," Clifford said, as he stood at the back of the toboggan. "Maybe I should buy your outfit."

We readily agreed, unable to imagine a better home for the dogs. That evening we were with Clifford and Lily as they surprised their daughter, Mika, with the news. Mika's face lit up with delight when she learned they had bought the entire team of dogs, as well as the toboggan and harnesses.

Clifford explained to her the responsibilities that went with owning a team of dogs. Until now, Mika had been training puppies and small dogs of various shapes and sizes. This was her first real team.

"Can I go in the race?" Mika asked. The annual spring dogsled race was only two days away, on March 21. Clifford smiled and nodded his agreement. Our freight team had just become a racing team.

On the morning of the race, we helped Mika hook Jeff, Blue, Buck, Tom, and Link to a borrowed racing sled.

I crossed my fingers, hoping they would not merely trot down the trail as we had trained them to do for our journey.

"Don't worry about him," Sally reassured Mika when Tom barked loudly as the excitement peaked. "He's really gentle once you get to know him."

A gunshot rang out and they were off! The dogs must have wondered what happened to the six-hundred-pound load they had been pulling for so long. With almost no weight behind them, they flew across the snow.

As the dogs came to the home stretch, we shared their excitement. Those were "our" dogs running so fast!

"Way to go, boys!" I called as they pulled Mika across the finish line.

The team placed in the top three, even though the other competitors had trained for racing all season. When the dogs stopped and stood with chests heaving, I knew the broad canine grins and wagging tails were a sign they had enjoyed themselves.

"I think they'll have a good life," Sally said after the dogs had hauled several other children along the race course. She petted Tom one last time. Our sadness at parting with the dogs was softened by the knowledge that they would be loved and cared for by the Carrière family.

That evening, the Carrières held a going-away party for Sally and me. Still wearing boots and parkas, we barbecued supper outside by the warmth of a bonfire. We felt at home as we ate broiled muskrat and dodged wood smoke. The best part of our day came when Lily brought out a cake with "Goodbye Ian and Sally" written in Cree across the top.

"Goodbye to you," Sally said. "It's been a wonderful winter!"

We left Cumberland House the next day with the smell of wood smoke lingering on our clothes and with memories of northern friends, both two-legged and four-legged, in our hearts.

"Je suis un homme du nord," I said to Sally, repeating the boast of a voyageur who had wintered in the North Country: I am a Northman.

"Et moi, je suis une femme du nord!" she proclaimed.

We had joined the ranks of the few Canadians who had paddled a birchbark canoe to a remote post and continued by dog team during winter. We understood why, despite the hardships, many paddlers had signed on for another year, or two, or three. There was freedom and adventure in the North Country. I knew that we, too, would return some day.

FROM THE AUTHORS

Thank you for joining us on our journey back in time. If you held your breath as we canoed down a set of rapids or put on a sweater when the temperature dropped to minus thirty, we accomplished our goal of bringing you with us.

Sally and I would like to invite you to share our other journeys. *Wilderness Seasons* is our story of living in the wilderness of northern British Columbia for fourteen months. Together, we built a log cabin and shared the trials and triumphs of life far from civilization. In *Wild and Free*, we tell of our experiences photographing wildlife in the north. Along the way, we were chased by angry bull elk, befriended by porcupines, and had several close encounters with bears and other wild creatures.

Arctic Adventures is the story of our year in the Arctic. We canoed across the Barrens and lived with an Inuit family during early winter, then travelled by dog team down the coast of Hudson Bay. And *Gold Rush* is our tale of reliving a year in the life of the gold-seekers of the Klondike one hundred years ago. From a packhorse trip, floating down the Yukon River in a hand-built scow, and moiling for gold, we tell of a year of adventure as Klondikers.

What's next? Once we've saved up a grubstake for another journey, we would like to step back to the days of the settlers who traversed the prairies by wagon train. For now, we will dream of covered wagons and strong horses, quiet evenings by campfires, and dusty trails. After all, dreams are where all journeys begin.

Ian and Sally Wilson, July 2000

ACKNOWLEDGEMENTS

We would like to thank our sponsors for their support. To all, we are most grateful for their financial assistance, for product contributions, and, most of all, for their faith in our expedition.

Altamira Investment Services for their financial contribution and their enthusiastic support of our expedition.

The North West Company for their sponsorship of our journey to relive the life of Nor'Westers.

Molson Breweries for their support and sponsorship of our endeavour.

The Royal Canadian Geographical Society for their contribution to our expedition.

Ralston Purina for contributing Pro Plan Dog Food that kept our seven hungry dogs fuelled for the long journey.

Far West Industries for their excellent Gore-Tex parkas, pants, and fleece jackets.

Cascade Designs for waterproof packs, Giardian water filters, and Therm-a-rest sleeping mats.

Coleman Canada for supplying us with Peak 1 camp stoves and lanterns.

We would also like to thank everyone who offered help and encouragement along the way. With their support our expedition was everything we hoped it would be. Among many others, we would like to thank the following:

Bob and Anne Wilson for being our expedition support crew.

Maureen Bayless for all her help with this book.

Joe and Lori Milligan for their help with our trip research and for their enthusiasm.

Tom Byers of Wood River Canoe Company in Lively, Ontario, for sharing his knowledge of birchbark canoe-making and for building a canoe with us that withstood the rigours of our journey.

Chris Gill and Laurie Thomson for joining us for a week of paddling and camaraderie.

Josh Robbins for help with photography in Voyageurs National Park.

Hal Murphy and the staff at Voyageurs National Park for their encouragement along the way.

Pam Hawley of Fort Frances for her support and a great rendezvous.

Judy McPherson and friends at the Manitoba Living History Society for a great rendezvous and feast on the Winnipeg River.

Derek Owen of Pinawa for help with photography.

John and Gloria Barnard of Lac du Bonnet for their hospitality.

Roger Batchelor of Beaconia for help with photography on Lake Winnipeg.

Clifford and Lily Carrière for their support, trail clearing, and hospitality while we were in Cumberland House.

John and Freda Carrière of Cumberland House for their advice and support.

Chip and Denise McKenzie and Fred and Elaine Hems of Cumberland House for their help with our dog team.

Anne Acco for putting up with snowshoe-building, dog-food-mixing, and other projects in the old convent at Cumberland House.

And, of course, all the other people of Cumberland House who made us feel so welcome during our winter stay.

John and Shirley Calvert for lending us a lead dog, offering dogsledding advice, and sharing their hospitality in The Pas.

Gordon Soules for his belief in our projects and unwavering support of our endeavours.

BIBLIOGRAPHY

Our voyageur experience was greatly enhanced by learning about the history of the fur trade before we embarked on our journey. Many of the historical quotations in the book come from Alexander Henry's *Travels and Adventures in Canada*, written almost two centuries ago. We hope that readers wishing to learn more will find the following material as helpful as we did.

Adney, Tappan. *The Bark Canoes and Skin Boats of North America*. Washington: Smithsonian Institution Press, 1983.

Henry, Alexander. *Travels and Adventures in Canada*. New York: I. Riley Publishers, 1809.

Morse, Eric W. *Fur Trade Canoe Routes of Canada*. Toronto: University of Toronto Press, 1969.

Nute, Grace Lee. *The Voyageur's Highway*. St. Paul, Minnesota: The Minnesota Historical Society, 1941.

Nute, Grace Lee. *The Voyageur*. St. Paul, Minnesota: The Minnesota Historical Society, 1955.

Silverston, Howard. *The Illustrated Voyageur*. Mount Horeb, Wisconsin: Midwest Traditions, 1996.

INDEX

Best-selling books by Ian and Sally Wilson

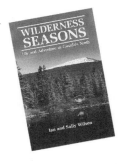

Wilderness Seasons is an inspiring account of a year in remote wilderness. From the challenge of building a hand-hewn log cabin to the intimacy of moose breath at six feet, the authors share the trials and triumphs of a life close to nature.

208 pages, ISBN 0-919574-34-3
$16.95

Wild and Free is a mix of photographs, drawings, and personal encounters with wildlife. Mountain climbing with goats, petting porcupines, and meeting burly black bears are just some of the adventures the authors share.

192 pages, ISBN 0-919574-87-4
$16.95

Arctic Adventures is the exciting story of a year-long adventure in the Arctic. The authors travelled 2000 miles by canoe and dog team, lived with an Inuit family, and learned how to build igloos and run a team of seven Huskies.

248 pages, ISBN 0-919574-43-2
$16.95

Gold Rush is an engaging story of a year reliving the Klondike adventure, from travelling by horseback, on foot, and by hand-built boat, to the excitement of finding gold!

248 pages, ISBN 0-919574-59-9
$16.95

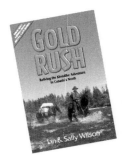

Published by Gordon Soules Book Publishers Ltd.